Don't You Quit!

The Magic of Untiring Efforts

NISHANT JAIN

First published in Hindi as *Ruk Jaana Nahin* in 2019 by Hind Yugm and Eka, an imprint of Westland Publications Private Limited

Published in English as *Don't You Quit!* in 2021 by Westland Publications Private Limited, in association with Hind Yugm

Published in English as *Don't You Quit!* in 2024 by Westland Books, a division of Nasadiya Technologies Private Limited

ISBN: 9789360452377

10 9 8 7 6 5 4 3 2 1

Typeset by Ashutosh Jha
Printed at Parksons Graphics Pvt. Ltd

Don't You Quit!

Every young mind has a dream, and it wishes to fulfill it and achieve success. Nishant Jain also nurtured this dream and, despite not coming from a privileged background, he fought against all odds and secured a high rank in the Union Public Service Examination. Before becoming IAS officer, he worked with the Parliament Secretariat for two years. He received his bachelor's and master's degrees from Meerut College and did M.Phil. from the University of Delhi. An IAS officer of the 2015 batch, Nishant Jain loves blogging and poetry.

In this motivational book, Jain has shared life lessons for personal and professional life. His valuable inputs on life skills, personality development, stress management and writing skills make this a unique book. Jain has also shared some tips for handling failures. Failure precedes success; it leads us to success if we accept it and learn from it. This book also features some inspiring success stories of UPSC aspirants who set an example by standing up to challenges and achieving their dreams.

Jain's bestselling book *All About UPSC Civil Services Exam* was an instant success among young readers. It is also available in Hindi and Marathi. His book *Ruk Jaana Nahin* has sold close to 20,000 copies and has consistently featured in the Amazon Best Reads list.

Nishant can be reached at:
nishantjainias@gmail.com
nishantjainias.blogspot.com

Don't you Quit....

— Nishant

Tarang Sinha is a writer and author. Her articles and stories have been published in magazines like *Good Housekeeping India*, *Child India*, *Woman's Era* and *New Woman*. She holds a Diploma in Creative Writing in English from IGNOU.

tarangsinha.blogspot.com

Dedicated to young minds

Contents

Preface

The idea of writing this book first occurred to me when I was at the World Book Fair in Delhi in 2018. Whenever I visit a book fair or a college, for that matter, I absolutely cherish the opportunity to interact with young minds. When these enthusiastic and talented people come up to me with their eyes gleaming in hope to learn something new, I feel overwhelmed by a sense of responsibility.

I court a lot of questions. 'How does one stay motivated despite the struggle?' 'How do I manage stress?' 'How to handle failures?' 'How do I develop an overall personality?'

Sometimes, when we chase our dreams, a sense of despair grips us. It's normal. Even I feel low at times. But there are certain tips and tricks that can help us overcome this phase. I have tried to gauge the psychological mindset of the youth and then help them with small and absolutely doable mantras and hacks. They are our future. They deserve great guidance and support.

I've written this book for students preparing for competitive exams, but these tips should help anyone willing to make small changes in their lives, personal or professional.

Becoming an IAS officer was my dream. So, between twenty-two and twenty-eight years of age, I appeared in different competitive exams, tasting success and failure in equal measure. Whether it was a Group C, a Group B or a Group A job, I moved towards my dream step by step. I persevered and remained steadfast all through to eventually live my dream. I want you to do the same.

There are several other things that make this book special and important. Along with effective and practical tips for personality development, it deals with time and stress management in a detailed yet interesting way. How can a slight change in your thought process make your life and career better? This book tells you that. It also talks about improving your reading and writing skills. Basically, it attempts to peek inside your confused and jumbled mind and provide you with practical, easily achievable solutions without being preachy.

I am grateful to Eka Westland for believing in my idea of presenting this book, originally published in Hindi as *Ruk Jaana Nahin*, to you. Mr Shailesh Bharatavasi of *Hind Yugm* appreciated and supported the concept. Very well received, *Ruk Jaana Nahin* also got featured in Amazon's bestsellers' list. Team Westland and Ms Amrita Talwar helped this book reach the target readers and I'm really thankful to them.

The phenomenal success of *Ruk Jaana Nahin* warranted an English edition. Westland Publications and Ms Minakshi Thakur helped me achieve that. I would also like to thank Tarang Sinha for her excellent translation. Also, thank you to my dear friends Abhishek Saraf, Abhishek Jain and Harish for their invaluable suggestions.

I extend heartfelt gratitude to my elder brother Prashant Jain (deputy editor, *Navbharat Times*) for his wonderful ideas, constant support and encouragement. I am very thankful to Suhani, my wife, for her patience and motivation. The smiling faces of my lovely nephew Aagam, niece Akshara and my naughty and adorable son Akshar have always been my inspiration.

Lastly, I would like to share these lines by Robert Frost that always inspire me to do something new and meaningful:

'The woods are lovely, dark and deep,
But I have promises to keep,
And miles to go before I sleep,
And miles to go before I sleep.'

1

How to groom your personality

Dreams are beautiful. They give you hope and courage. So many young small-town people, with dreams nestling in their hearts, move to big cities every day, away from their dear ones, to try their luck, hoping to create a better life for themselves. But it's not easy to just move to a bigger city and achieve success, is it? So what should they do to improve their probability of success?

Our personality and behaviour play important roles in the journey of our life and success, no matter what we do. So, what changes should young talented candidates adopt to make their dreams come true?

Do these questions often bother you? Bear with me then as I try to help you with my limited knowledge and experience.

There's no doubt that some positive and effective changes in our personality can increase the possibility of our success. Here I would like to point out a few things:

Keep your enthusiasm alive

There are so many examples of eminent people battling challenges with their courage and passion, carving a path for themselves. A path that led them to their destination. Famous poet **Edgar Guest** wrote:

'When things go wrong, as they sometimes will,
When the road you're trudging seems all uphill,
When the funds are low and the debts are high,
And you want to smile, but you have to sigh,
When care is pressing you down a bit,
Rest if you must—but don't you quit.'

The degree of passion and exhilaration should be so strong that nothing can deter us from creating our own path.

We should keep in mind that our deep attachment with something or someone makes us weak. Ever experienced this? We must ensure that we start our journey without any strong attachment or expectations. It's hard, no doubt, but when you expect less and move on without waiting for an instant result, you are less likely to be disappointed. You keep working hard and the possibility of your success increases. Unexpected and positive results are so exciting! Aren't they?

Moreover, it saves us from unnecessary pressure and nagging stress. Please understand that our performance improves when we are relaxed.

Life has a very strict rule: it goes on, no matter what. Excuses don't work. We have to work. Even if we are not able to reach our destination, we need to keep moving towards the right direction. Because success is a journey, not a destination.

Have faith in yourself

I have been a student and an aspirant. So I know that this phase of exam preparation can be really tiring. So tiring and time-consuming that we might lose enthusiasm at times. We may begin to doubt our ability. We might start thinking, 'Have I chosen the right path? Am I going in the right direction?'

The good thing is it's natural and totally fine. It shows that you're trying really hard. However, not everyone can handle this stress and self-doubt. They unintentionally create a bubble of negativity around themselves. Every aspect of competitive exams begins to stress them out. It can trigger a battle with the negative inner voice that says, 'I won't get selected'; 'I'm not good enough'; 'I can't write my answers well' or 'What if I go blank in the examination hall?'

Whenever I reminiscence about my past, I realise that I had never questioned my ability. I truly believed in our examination system, my subject and, most importantly, myself! And that's why I can say that self-belief can play a pivotal role in cracking competitive exams. Self-belief backs confidence and widens your horizon.

Recognize your potential and move ahead

Nature has gifted us with something very special—talent. Sometimes it's hidden and people take some time or motivation to recognise it. But have you ever noticed that everyone always excels at something unique? Interesting, isn't it?

We all have some shortcomings. However, we also have the capability to overcome these shortcomings if we start working on them. But can we make things better if we keep thinking that everything is already good and doesn't need improvement? No. You can't work on your faults until you accept them. **Acceptance** is necessary as a step ahead in this journey. So is **introspection**.

But the thing is, introspection is a tad tricky. Preaching is the easiest thing to do in the entire world; following the insights isn't. Even preachers fail to recognise and accept their own shortcomings. There's a simple, psychological reason behind this. We enjoy the company of people who appreciate us and conveniently ignore our faults. Not everyone can be like Kabir, you see, who had the courage to respect his own critics.

Remember what **Kabir** had said?

'Nindak niyre rakhiye, aangan kuti chhavaay.'

(Keep your critics in your close vicinity so that they can remind you that you're not perfect.)

A poet, **Pandit Daulat Ram**, has described the characteristic of great people in an interesting way. He says, 'Great people have the tendency to hide two things—their own merits and someone else's demerits.'

Embrace your faults in the way **Dr Nawaz Deobandi**, an Urdu poet, expresses so beautifully:

'Jis mein khud ke bheetar ke bhi aib dikhai dete ho,
Humne aisa bhi ek apna chashma banwa rakha hai.'

(I've bought a pair of magical spectacles through which I can spot my own shortcomings.)

Besides, our personality should essentially have **the skill to identify our strengths and weaknesses**.

If we enjoy praise, we must have the courage to accept criticism as well. It's as simple as that. This constructive criticism gives us homework—to work on our own flaws.

Shaandaar, zabardast, zindabad!

I'm sure you have heard of the supremely diligent Dashrath Manjhi, an iconic man from Bihar who carved a path through a hill using only a hammer and a chisel. The movie based on his life, *Manjhi–The Mountain Man*, has portrayed his passion and determination beautifully.

One aspect of his determination stands out in particular. Whenever someone tried to demotivate him, Manjhi would chant, '*Shaandaar, zabardast, zindabad!*' (Magnificent, tremendous, eternal!) Indeed, what he did was truly magnificent, tremendous and, of course, eternal.

There's an insightful quote by **Shiv Khera**: 'Winners don't do different things. They do things differently.'

Consistency is powerful. People who achieve their goals are usually consistent in their efforts. You might have noticed that people usually start with a bang. They seem determined and enthusiastic but most are unable to keep the spark alive. They seem incapable of tackling troubles.

Blaming others for your own troubles or mistakes is one of the easiest things to do, isn't it? This is exactly what some people do. They try to stay safe by choosing the easiest option.

Browse through the success stories of achievers or toppers of competitive exams and they have something common—**persistence**. You need to keep that in mind.

However, the methods of gauging talent or ability have changed over time. Earlier, **intelligence quotient (IQ)** used to be the benchmark, but now **emotional quotient (EQ)** has also become an important parameter. Your mental state matters. And these days, two new terms have evolved—**adversity quotient (AQ)** and **persistence** or **perseverance quotient (PQ)**.

IQ represents the ability to learn or understand, which is the ratio of the mental age to the chronological age multiplied by hundred or a score determined by comparing one's performance to the average scores in one's age group.

EQ means the ability to perceive, assess and manage the emotions of one's self and of others, including:

- Identifying emotions
- Evaluating and perceiving how others feel

- Controlling one's own emotions
- Using emotions to facilitate social communication
- Relating to others

AQ is the ability to face and overcome changes and adversities while turning them into opportunities for greater achievement. It comprises four CORE dimensions:

C = Control
O = Ownership
R = Reach
E = Endurance

People with high AQ perceive themselves with significant control in adverse situations, holding themselves accountable for dealing with various situations, overcoming setbacks with courage and staying positive.

Suppose you have been assigned a project. You are full of energy and enthusiasm when you start, but then your energy dwindles. What would be the result? The project would be less likely to succeed. Similarly, you need to be consistent while you are preparing for an exam. You need to keep your enthusiasm and energy high. Your AQ and PQ play very important roles here.

The importance of consistency has been expressed wonderfully in this poem by **Sohan Lal Dwivedi**. This is a poem Amitabh Bachchan recites often:

'Jab tak na safal ho, neend chain ko tyaago tum,
Sangharsho ka maidaan chhor mat bhago tum,
Kuch kiye bina hi jai-jaikaar nahi hoti,
Koshish karne walo ki kabhi haar nahi hoti.'

(Don't rest, until you achieve your aim,
Don't give up, just because it's a tough game.
Without diligence, you can't savour victory.
Remember, nothing can beat you, if you try
wholeheartedly.)

Keep learning

Humans have a quality that makes us powerful—it is our hunger to learn. And it's our hunger to learn and experiment that has led us to the path of inventions and discoveries.

Even a child has this fervent tendency to learn through an interesting medium called imitation.

Learning is wonderful. It's a never-ending journey, and there are so many interesting and insightful mediums that act as tools for learning—people around us, a casual conversation, the environment, newspapers, books, the internet, magazines, our own experiences, failures and what not. Anything, anyone, any day can be a teacher.

We think, we learn and eventually attain a level of maturity and understanding in life.

Age and maturity are two different things, and sometimes they have nothing to do with each other. Isn't it strange? That's life for you!

Now, let's talk about career and success. The UPSC Civil Service examination and many other prestigious competitive exams require a certain level of maturity. Interestingly, this maturity has nothing to do with your age. You might have noticed that sometimes a youngster has got balanced views and a deep understanding of things, whereas a fifty-year-old person can exhibit an immature demeanour. Our **maturity, understanding and keenness to learn** are crucial for attaining and maintaining success.

Just like learning, **knowledge is never-ending. It's like a vast ocean of which we have tasted only a few drops**. However, these few drops are precious and exclusively ours. Nobody can steal that from us.

Learning is an opportunity. Do not hesitate even if you get this opportunity from youngsters and less experienced people. Be open-minded. Be a keen observer. Learning is important, the source isn't. It's not just about doing well in certain competitive exams; it's also about doing well in life. Your hunger to learn creates a base for self-development.

The prolific poet **Bhavani Prasad Mishra** has beautifully said:

'Kuch likh kar so, kuch padh kar so,
Tu jis jagah jaga savere, us jagah se badhkar so.'

(Write something before you go to sleep,
Read something before you go to sleep,
Be sure you make some progress,
From morning till you go to sleep.)

Attitude and aptitude

They say, '**Love what you do, and do what you love**.' They're absolutely right! Can you imagine giving your hundred per cent if you don't enjoy what you are doing? No. So, if you want to succeed in a particular field, ask yourself certain questions—'Does it interest me? Do I find it fascinating?' Make sure the answer is yes. If you enjoy what you're doing, it means it comes naturally to you. It enhances the probability of your success.

We are in the age of specialisation. If you want to be a manager, you will be tested on your management skills. If you want to be a teacher or a researcher, your teaching/research aptitude will be under the scanner.

However, if I talk with special reference to the UPSC Civil Services exam, it's unique in terms of 'testing' your skills. It does not expect you to be a specialist. It expects you to be a generalist. Instead of testing your expertise in a certain field, it tests your basic views and understanding about life, society and the environment.

You can say it is the basic nature of the Civil Services; they look for young visionaries and chisel their skills.

In the course of continuous development of attitude and aptitude, you need to keep certain things in mind:

1. Be aware and stay updated. Keep track of current affairs. What's happening around the world, in terms of social, cultural and political dimensions? Make sure you know that.

2. Make social concerns a part of your daily life. How can you contribute to society? What can you do for the people in need? Savour the joy of giving.
3. Common sense is one of the greatest qualities. When in a state of dilemma, use your common sense. However, common sense is not very common, you see. Or I should say, people fail to use it when most needed. If you use your common sense properly, it can guide you smartly.
4. Narrowmindedness narrows the possibility to learn. So, embrace new thoughts and ideas.

It has been mentioned in the **Rig Veda**:

'Aa no bhadra kratvo yantu vishvtaha.'

(Let noble thoughts come to us from every side.)

So, don't be a slave to a narrow mind. Keep your thoughts and visions balanced, and your personality will prosper.

There's no substitute for hard work

There's an old saying:

'Karat karat abhyaas te jadmati hot sujaan.
Rasri aawat-jaat te, sil par padat nisaan.'

(Even a foolish person can become wise with regular practice, just like that persistent rope that carves a mark with constant friction at the well.)

In simple words, there's no substitute for hard work and regular practice. There's no shortcut to success. You need to keep going. Take rest if you feel tired but never stop if you want to reach your destination.

Remember, hard work is crucial. Not just to achieve success, but to maintain it in the long journey of your career. Hurdles are inevitable. It's their tendency to keep bugging you. Only your continuous hard work can keep these hurdles in check. Someone has said, '**The prize for hard work is more hard work.**'

Sounds confusing? Let me elaborate. Laziness can give you pleasure for some time. But in the long run, it's your hard work that would make you successful and happy.

Politeness is the best policy

In the process of personality development, it's important to develop a quality: politeness.

Politeness is a feel-good virtue that makes you happy and others comfortable. Don't tell me that you haven't met someone who turns arrogant the moment he achieves success.

We must learn to cherish whatever happiness life gifts us but it's not a very good idea to allow success go to your head to such an extent that you take pleasure in demeaning others. You don't rise by dragging others down but by lifting yourself up. You may not realise it but belittling others doesn't make you superior.

And why this arrogance? If you think you know everything then you are mistaken. There's so much to learn, so many things we don't know. There's an interesting theory: How can you show growth in a small line without making any changes? By drawing a bigger line next to it. Be that bigger line, not for others but for yourself, and keep growing.

Develop your skills

Although we have unlimited capability, how do we categorise people? How do we decide if a particular person is capable or not? The benchmark is the 'skill' that person exhibits. Have you started thinking it's going to be difficult? Already? Hold on. Interestingly, you can develop your skills easily. You just need some dedication and yes, hard work.

What are the basic skills we are talking about here? Skills are basically categorised into three groups:

1. **Technical skills**
2. **Conceptual skills**
3. **Human skills**

If we talk with reference to competetive exams, our knowledge, practice, strategy, revision, etc. would fall under technical skills. Our opinions on various topics, our understanding, interpretation, etc. would fall under conceptual skills and our passion for life and learning, our attitude and aptitude would fall under human skills.

For thorough personality development, we need to develop all these skills. So the youth, their minds full of dreams, ideas and hope, should try to instil all these skills in themselves.

Writing skills: How to express yourself

Popular philosopher **Francis Bacon** had said: 'Reading makes a full man, conference a ready man and writing an exact man.'

If we really want to improve our speaking, reading and writing skills, we must have a good command of the language in question. When I say 'a good **command of the language**', I don't mean you should use difficult words or complex sentences. What I mean is that you should express yourselves clearly and smartly. Write right. Write to the point. Your sentences should be crisp and succinct. That's all.

How to develop your writing skills? There's a very simple answer: **Practise and keep practising**. There could be two aspects of developing better writing skills:

1. What to write
2. How to write

What to write? The answer to this question lies in the reading and understanding of the questions carefully. I'm sure your teachers or elders have told you once in a while to read the question paper carefully. That's important. When you read and comprehend the question carefully, it actually guides you towards the answer. And if you write your answers in a clean and systematic manner, you are bound to get good scores.

How to write? It is as important as 'what to write'. Let me share some useful tips:

1. Always write in a clear and organised manner.
2. Learn to develop a flow and lucidity in your writing. Write in small paragraphs. Make sure that two consecutive paragraphs are connected. It creates a flow.
3. Use simple and coherent words and sentences. Difficult/unusual words or irrelevant sentences fail to make an impression. It makes your answers look forced. Please avoid that. Don't use four sentences to tell something that can be said in a single sentence. Be crisp and concise.
4. If possible, don't hesitate to use examples, quotations, data or anecdotes. It makes your answers more interesting and authentic. Just make sure that they are relevant and in sync with the topic you are discussing.
5. Please understand that your command of the language and lucidity in your writing won't develop overnight. It needs practice and time. So be patient. Start practising today. Don't push it to tomorrow. **Tomorrow never comes.**

If you follow these tips, they might become your strength. Use your strength and recognise your potential. If you don't trust your own abilities, nobody else will. So if you have any kind of inferiority complex, crush it right away! You lose a battle if your heart and mind have already accepted defeat. It's better you understand this early in your life. Your confidence and psychological strength are powerful tools. They can help you win the different battles of life.

Nurture relationships

Learn to cherish and value relationships. They support you in life and in the process of preparation. Your friends and family motivate you, fill you with energy. They lift your spirits when you feel a little low. So, no matter how busy you are, make time for those who really care. I had heard this line somewhere—'*Laakh mushquil zamaane mein hai, rishte to bas nibhane mein hai.*'

The gist of this quote is that there may be many troubles in life but you can overcome them only if you nurture and value your relationships. They are your real assets.

During exam preparations or while dealing with the humdrum of life, it's a little impractical to think everything will go smoothly. Just like life, preparing for any competitive exam is full of ups and downs. Exam preparation cannot go in a straight line, you see. And it can make you weak or nervous at times, which is okay. But in these weak moments, you need a hand of assurance, some words of affection. Who better than your family and friends for this?

An endearing conversation, a hearty laugh and the sense of togetherness make you stress-free. It relaxes your nerves and acts as a soothing balm to your tired mind. It's natural. Everybody needs it. So cherish those moments to recharge yourself.

Optimism and positivity: The game changers

Have you ever known anyone who just cannot stop whining? It doesn't help, to be honest. I have realised that your positivity and hopeful approach can make things a little easier. However, understandably, it's not easy to keep your optimism and motivation under control all the time. Sometimes they slip off. What can you do to prevent it?

1. Try to be happy and make others happy. Don't overthink, try to enjoy your studies and life. A poet has rightly said: '*Na khud raho, na kisi ko udaas rehne do*'. (Don't be sad, and don't let others stay sad.) Isn't it lovely? So, can you do that?
2. Celebrate happiness and achievements, no matter how small they are. Don't reserve today's happiness for tomorrow. What I mean to say is, don't wait for a bigger achievement or happiness. Joyful moments are precious. Small or big, it doesn't matter.
3. We have so many people in our lives. Some people motivate us but some others give negative vibes. Try to be with people who reflect positive energy and

encourage you. Keep distance from negative and misleading people. We don't need unnecessary stress, do we? However, don't ignore constructive criticism. Don't take it personally. It acts as a tonic for your growth.

4. Develop hobbies. Maybe you don't really need to develop them. We all have some kinds of interests. Think about it. Do you like sports, or maybe playing certain indoor games? Or reading novels? Watching movies? Hanging out with friends? Listening to music? Spend some time doing that. It can boost your morale and rejuvenate your mind to start afresh. Say life offers you joy and stress—which one would you choose? The choice is yours.

Set small goals, start celebrating small achievements and don't be stressed about small mistakes.

2

While being super busy, stay organised and cool

A gentleman, let's call him Mr A, is a devoted student focused on his career and determined to clear the competitive exams. He's so engrossed in the preparation that he hardly gets time to eat or even sleep. His tiny study room is full of bookshelves stuffed with various kinds of books. Piles of notes are strewn all over his study table. His dedication won't give you career goals but would make you terribly stressed.

However, surprisingly, Mr A hasn't cracked any competitive exam yet. Baffling, but true.

His close friends say that although he's hardworking and dedicated, he studies in a haphazard manner. And he's terribly tense during exams.

Another gentleman, Mr B, is sorted. He usually keeps himself busy in studies but he isn't a recluse. He knows that you need to make time for important things and friends.

No wonder he's popular and everyone's favourite. A guy with a good sense of time management always is.

Do you realise that Mr A and Mr B don't seem to be fictional characters? They're in fact the boys next door. We all have come across such people, right? So tell me one thing. And answer honestly, okay?

Have you ever felt that your hard work and dedication don't yield fruitful results? Ever felt that your life is a maze of jumbled thoughts? Ever wondered why a certain friend or acquaintance has succeeded while success eludes you? You're smart. You work hard. Then why aren't you succeeding?

If you find yourself nodding to these questions, you need an extensive self-analysis. Maybe you're Mr A. Maybe, your unorganised behaviour is the main problem.

It's not a journey that you need to accomplish but a simple and casual walk from Mr A to Mr B. That's it. No journey is a cakewalk but you need to understand that there's a difference between walking on a path, however difficult, and wandering inside a labyrinth.

There's something about being organised. It uplifts your mood.

It's not just about working hard and always staying busy. It's also about working wisely and channelising your energy in a smart way.

Now, let us discuss the benefits of being organised and relaxed while being super busy:

- You're usually happy and full of positive energy.

- Whatever you read, you enjoy. That's how you develop an ability to remain calm even in a stressful situation.
- Your ability to stay composed helps you perform better in the examination hall or interview room because your mind rejects unnecessary baggage and you write the answers or speak with a stress-free mind.
- Moreover, you are not too anxious about the results because you are prepared to face any situation. There's an old saying, **'Try for the best, prepare for the worst.'**

Actually, it's a blessing to be an easy-going person. It's fantastic if you manage to be busy and relaxed at the same time. Staying busy fills you with a sense of satisfaction and you are able to make your day productive.

All you have to do is make certain changes in your habits so that you can be busy and happy at the same time. What are those changes?

- Try to lead a routine life. It doesn't mean your days have to be perfect. Perfect routine is a myth. Make a decent, doable timetable and stick to it.
- If you have the habit of being unorganised, it won't go away overnight. Don't try to change your routine drastically or too quickly. Go slow. Create a schedule. Apart from regular studies, make sure writing, practising and revision find their much-needed spots in this schedule.

- Be relaxed. Take care of your health and hygiene. And don't forget your hobbies. It would be wonderful if you could practice yoga and pranayam.
- Keeping yourself busy makes you fit, physically as well as mentally. Remember, staying happy and studying in a relaxed manner has its own charm.
- Joy is infectious. So be joyful. Don't just look happy; be happy in the truest sense. Only then would you be able to create a joyful environment around yourself.

3

The joy of giving and helping others

Life is a winding path, full of ups and downs, hardships and adversities. You make efforts to make things right, but hurdles don't leave you alone and that's the moment you ask yourself, 'Why me?' Frankly, hurdles are inevitable. You are being delusional if you expect your path to be easy. Sometimes you expect your close ones to help you rectify the errors in your life. You feel if your friends and family had helped you, life would have been in a better shape. Have you ever thought like this?

Knowledge and experiences are like an ocean, vast and unfathomable. Our life, in terms of knowledge and experience, can be summarised as a couple of dives in that ocean. The famous Greek philosopher **Socrates** had said, 'The only true wisdom is in knowing you know nothing.' Realising that you have tasted 'just a few drops' from this ocean of knowledge makes you wise.

Perhaps we are not as enlightened as Socrates. However, we do know that it's impossible to attain the most knowledgeable state, don't we? The place, time and circumstances have their own limitations. We cannot be present in every era, place or circumstance, can we? So, we need to remember that we cannot be the most knowledgeable in the entire world.

'*Parasparopagraho jeevanam*'—the Jain saint **Uma Swami** has mentioned this term in the text *Tatwarth Sutra*. It means: **Living beings benefit by helping each other**.

If you follow this mantra, it can help you in various stages of life as well as in exam preparation.

While preparing for any exam, students often think that their knowledge is exclusive. They don't like to share their knowledge. They think that if they share their notes, the other person would get more marks.

Friends, understand that this is a highly conservative mindset, a thought that sprouts from a narrow mind. And it's not going to help you.

As I mentioned earlier, the nature of the Civil Services exam is unique. And I say this from personal experience. Your ability is gauged from your own extensive study, common sense and talent. Merely following anyone won't make any difference. So, if you're that conservative person who hesitates to share knowledge, you are just being insecure. It means you don't believe in your own ability. Remember what I said earlier? Self-belief is crucial.

The examination pattern has somehow changed or evolved over time. And I would say that adopting the philosophy of *parasparopagraho jeevanam* is quite practical in this new pattern of examination. In fact, it can make your preparation more extensive and dynamic.

Let's take an example. As I said, nobody can be perfect. So suppose you have a better understanding in a certain field or segment, and your friend is more knowledgeable in another subject; you both can learn from each other and do better. That's why **group discussion** is important. Group discussions don't just enhance your knowledge; they can also make you a good speaker and a listener. Now, when it comes to discussion, you can't do it alone without sharing your knowledge, can you? Knowledge is a treasure but it shouldn't be kept only to yourself.

Haven't you heard that knowledge is wealth that grows by sharing?

And it's fascinating to share your knowledge. During my preparation days, I often felt like discussing what I had learnt with my friends. Psychology says, if you tell something to someone or hear something from someone, your brain stores that information for a longer period. It's the power of discussion. It stays with you. Discussion widens your horizon. It helps you see your own understanding in a new light.

There's a saying by Benjamin Franklin: 'Tell me and I forget. Teach me and I remember. Involve me and I learn'.

Parasparograho jeevanam, or the joy of helping each other, is not only beneficial for preparation, but it also helps you cope with the struggles and the tiresome process of preparation. It lifts your morale.

I've known some people who couldn't handle the stress and initial failures and got trapped in a web of depression and despair. It is okay if you want to stay alone and concentrate on your studies. But being a complete recluse can be a little problematic for you.

Everybody needs someone who can understand and listen to them. Suppressed emotions can be suffocating. And if it goes on for a longer period, it can affect you psychologically—in a negative way, of course.

It's a two-way street—when you help others and behave pleasantly with people, you receive, well, usually, a similar kind of treatment.

So learn to walk together. Even our scriptures endorse this theory. As it is mentioned in the **Rig Veda**:

> *'San gachhadhwam, san vadadhwam, san vo manansi jaantaam.'*
>
> (Walk together, speak together and try to understand others' feelings.)

If you go a little deeper, you would realise how important it is to help and support each other. And it is particularly crucial for students who are preparing for competitive exams. Sometimes even a stranger turns out to be a guardian angel. Sometimes you feel distracted, like a wandering soul, and then some people's support, an enlightening conversation or their assurance can guide you through the tough phase.

And have you ever realised how immensely joyful it is when your little help makes a big difference to somebody's life? **'Little drops of water make the mighty ocean.'** It doesn't cost much to be kind and nice. It has been rightly said, 'Kindness doesn't cost a thing; sprinkle it everywhere.' Let's try to create a cheerful and vivacious environment and experience a revolutionary change.

4

What are you reading these days?

'What are you reading these days?' one fine evening I asked my friend.

'Oh, I just finished *Indian Polity* by M. Laxmikanth. Currently I'm reading this magazine, *Yojana*, and I just bought the latest edition of the *India Yearbook*,' he finished in a single breath.

I couldn't help smiling. 'Apart from text or competitive books, I mean,' I said.

'Oh,' he managed to say, looking utterly confused as if I had asked an absurd question. You might be thinking that I spent a boring evening with a boring friend. No. It turned out to be a really interesting evening. What did we talk about? What did he say about books, other than those he read? Let me share something interesting with you.

Well, it's not unusual to restrict yourself within the boundaries of things related to exams and preparations. It happens. Most students do this, thinking that reading novels or entertainment magazines is a total waste of time. They view it as a betrayal, like a breach of promise they made to themselves in their attempt to crack a particular competition.

While it's valid and sensible that for better results, you need to be focused and free from distractions when you are preparing for competitive exams, I'd like to add that considering the new trend and pattern, the habit of reading has evolved as an important hobby. Wondering how? Let's discuss.

You might have noticed that the questions of the Civil Services exam have turned real only recently. It's difficult to predict how diverse or even erratic the source of the questions can be. It means that your preparation should be equally diverse. So, how would you do that? Restricting yourself to the regular competitive books means limiting your knowledge. You need to keep your mind, eyes and ears alert to gather all kinds of information.

If you want to improve your writing skills, you primarily need two things: good content and command of the language. Style and vocabulary play a significant role in attainting command of the language. Your habit of reading can act as a great helping hand in this process. If you're an avid reader, you would know that reading is a pleasure and a learning experience. Reading, other than text books, can build your command of the language.

Like any other hobby, reading is entertaining and full of wonders. But the question is—**how to find time for reading** good books, and what to read?

The answer to the first question is quite simple. Whenever you feel like taking a break from your rigorous studies, or whenever you are free or maybe travelling, read a book that interests or fascinates you. It can be a magazine or a recently released novel.

The second question—**what to read**—is a thought-provoking and not-so-simple question. So, I'll try to find the answer for you.

When it comes to reading novels or books other than text books, you can categorise them into **three or four categories**.

The first category: Books that do not fall under any study material, but you can learn a lot from them as they are written in a way that can widen your thoughts or vision. These are **non-fiction** books based on politics, economics, history, sciences, society, philosophy, etc. If you like such books, you can read Amartya Sen, Shashi Tharoor, Ramachandra Guha, Gurcharan Das, Rajni Kothari, Bipin Chandra, Ram Ahuja, Yuval Noah Harari, etc.

You can easily find all these books on websites like Amazon or Flipkart. Books by National Book Trust (NBT) or Publications Division (Government of India) can also be an option if you want to read such informative books.

The other category is **classics** or **literary fiction** that are rich in terms of language and prose. They can make you understand the complexities of life and society, and the psychology of interesting characters. Reading such books would make you more sensitive and sensible.

In the literary fiction category, you can read Jhumpa Lahiri, Chitra Banerjee Divakaruni, R.K. Narayan, Khaled

Hosseini, Vikram Seth, Anita Desai, etc. In classics, you can pick Jane Austen books to start with, *Rebecca* by Daphne Du Maurier if you like mystery, *To Kill a Mockingbird* by Harper Lee (a story based on racism), *1984* by George Orwell and short stories by Roald Dahl or P.G.Wodehouse if you enjoy humour.

If you enjoy **poetry**, you can read Sylvia Plath, Robert Frost, Emily Dickinson, Maya Angelou, F. Scott Fitzgerald, Tyler Knott Gregson, Noor Unnahar, etc. You may also enjoy English translations of famous Hindi/Urdu poets or lyricists like Gulzar, Bashir Badr, Nida Fazli, Javed Akhtar, Kumar Vishwas, Prasoon Joshi, Manoj Muntashir and Irshad Kamil.

Another category is **light fiction**, i.e., novels that are written by young authors keeping young readers in mind. They can be novels (of various genres, including mythology), novellas, anthologies or even travelogues. Young readers find them relatable and so such books are instant bestsellers, e.g., books by authors like Amish Tripathi, Ashwin Sanghi, Christopher C. Doyle, Chetan Bhagat, Anand Neelakantan and Devdutt Pattanaik.

One more interesting category these days is **self-help**. These books help us live a better and meaningful life. Some good books could be *The Subtle Art of Not Giving a F*ck* by Mark Manson, *The Art of Thinking Clearly* by Rolf Dobelli, *Man's Search for Meaning* by Viktor Frankl, *The Secret* by Rhonda Byrne, *Life's Amazing Secrets* by Gaur Gopal Das and *Ikigai* by Hector Garcia and Francesc Miralles. The book which you are reading right now also belongs to the same genre.

Apart from books, you can pick some magazines as well, like *India Today* or *Outlook*.

To encourage the book culture in India, several literary festivals are being organised these days. You can visit such festivals to experience the joy of reading and writing. They have quite a different and refreshing aura. You can browse, let your mind wander for a change, touch and feel books, and, of course, pick up whatever you like.

So what I'm trying to say is that **reading is a wonderful habit**. It enlightens you, transforms your views, widens your insights and gives you a better exposure. Besides, it tightens your grip over the language.

To ace any competitive exam, it is not essential to read the above-mentioned books. It's about your taste and choice. Having a hobby is a good thing. You never know when and how the words you savoured as a hobby might turn out to be an unexpected, shining bulb in your success journey and your life.

So, from now on, ask your friends, 'What are you reading these days?' and see what they say. It would be interesting, no?

5

The depth of knowledge: Surface level or deep?

Before discussing this topic, I'll tell you a story.

A long time ago, four Brahmin friends lived in a village. When they were small, they decided to study and gain some knowledge. They went to a town called Kannauj to study at a gurukul. They ignored the outer world and studied religiously for twelve years, garnering all the knowledge they could from various scriptures.

One day they realised that they had learned enough and now they should go home. They asked for permission from their teacher and left.

On the way back home, they found a trifurcated road. They looked at each other, not knowing which path to choose. They sat down to discuss and decide. One of the friends took out his manuscript and started looking for the answer.

Coincidentally, someone had died in a nearby village and people were taking the body to the crematorium. Right then, one of the boys found the answer in the manuscript: '*Mahajano yen gata sa pantha.*' It means it is difficult to understand the right path, so follow the path of the great people. They noticed people walking in a line following someone. Without understanding the actual meaning of the quote, they instantly decided that it was the caravan of a leader and started following them to the crematorium.

When they reached the crematorium, they saw a donkey. Having lived in isolation for twelve years, they had never seen any animal before. 'Which creature is this?' one of the boys asked.

Again, they found the answer in their manuscript:

'Utsave vyasane prapte durbhikshe shatrusankate
Rajdware shamshane cha yah tishthati sa bandhavah.'

(Those who stand by you in joy and sorrow, in famine, in fighting against your enemy, in getting justice and in the 'crematorium' [bad times] are your real friends.)

The boy read out the shloka and declared the donkey as their true friend. They embraced and patted the donkey.

As they were busy developing a bond of friendship with the donkey, a camel passed by. They were utterly surprised to see such a strange creature. 'Now, what's that? How swiftly it walks!' one of them whispered in awe. Again their famous manuscript came to their rescue, with '*Dharmasya twarita gatih.*' (Dharma travels fast.) Of course, according to them, that camel was Dharma. Another quote flashed in one of the boys' mind. He didn't need the manuscript this time. How learned he was! '*Ishtam dharmen yojyet,*' he remembered. (Connect the dear one [or a thing dear to you] with Dharma.)

Yup, you guessed it! They tied the donkey with the camel.

Someone complained to the master of the donkey and he came running with a rod. The boys managed to escape somehow.

Huffing and puffing, they reached a river. 'How to cross this river?' one of them asked.

They saw a leaf floating in the river. One of the boys suddenly remembered: '*Aagamishyati yatpatram tatpaaram taaryishyati.*' (When in trouble, seek help from anything you find. Even a leaf can help you cross the river, you never know.)

Now the manuscript cannot be wrong, can it? So, the one who remembered the shloka jumped over the floating leaf. Do I need to mention what happened next?

Well, they didn't know how to swim and the boy was about to drown. One of them clutched his locks but soon realised that he couldn't be saved. Suddenly, he slashed his head. Bewildered, the other two looked at him. The boy, his friend's head hanging in his hand, said, 'Don't you remember what we had read in the book?' He looked at his friends incredulously. 'If you seem to be losing everything, you must try to save something.'

Something is better than nothing. Sure!

Now just three in number, they reached a village. People used to respect Brahmins. So when the villagers came to know that they were Brahmins, the boys were invited for lunch.

The first boy went to a house where they served him vermicelli. The Brahmin boy immediately recalled what he had read: '*Dirghasootri vinashyati.*' (A procrastinator or a lazy person cannot succeed.) But the boy took it literally. He thought that if he ate a filamentous vermicelli, he would never be able to succeed. So he left the food untouched and departed.

The other Brahmin boy went to a place where he was served rotis. This time, he racalled a quote: '*Ativistaar visteernam tad bhavet na chirayusham*'. (Excessively expanded things don't have a long life.)

The flat, expanded rotis were giving him the jitters. He quickly excused himself, his platter untouched.

The third Brahmin got vada. He was reminded of '*Chhidreshvanartha bahuli bhavanti.*' (The drain increases in size if there's a hole.) In simpler words, a hole (weakness) invites troubles. The hole in the vada seemed to be gaping at the Brahmin boy. So he decided not to eat the food, and left.

They all remained hungry. People were sniggering at their foolishness but the Brahmin lads thought that people were impressed at their immense knowledge.

Hungry and tired, they finally reached their village. Upon hearing their story, Swarnasiddhi said, 'It's good to learn the manuscript, but you must have practical knowledge and understanding. Otherwise you may look like a fool, even though you are highly learned.'

This story is from the ancient Indian collection of fables, **Panchatantra**. Panchatantra has numerous fascinating tales, full of lessons. This story might seem exaggerated to you, but one cannot ignore the lesson it provides—a lesson that come handy in real life and in exam preparations as well.

Let's discuss.

You might have heard idioms like '**reading between the lines**' or '**in black and white**'. The first one means 'to understand the essence of a statement', not just the words that have been used to say it. The next idiom means 'a coherent expression'.

In the current world, 'reading between the lines' seems more significant and practical. Nothing is black and white these days. Everything has a hidden purpose or agenda, something like 'conditions apply'.

What I mean to say is, learning by heart or reading word-by-word without understanding the real meaning or message is not a very wise idea. You should be able to grasp the underlying message in a statement, not just the literal meaning of the words.

Be it the Civil Services exam or any other competitive exam, most have changed or evolved over time in terms of pattern and approach. You would realise that 'learning by heart' does not work anymore. What works now is '**understanding the gist**'. Whether it's academics or the basic study of current affairs, or your understanding in essay writing or even your balanced ethical views on any matter, everything requires practical understanding, apart from the learned knowledge.

Let's try to understand it in an easier way so that it can enhance the chances of your success. We will go pointwise to make it simple:

1. Whenever you start reading a new topic or subject for the first time, read it casually, without any pressure of gaining deep knowledge.
2. Try to highlight the portions that seem significant. Make sure you don't overdo it.
3. Whenever you come across a new terminology or concept, take notes and try to understand it separately. You may use sites like Wikipedia on the internet or any reference book as your helping hand.

Reading and grasping are two different things. The process of learning doesn't go in a straight line. It includes thinking, revising, discussing and listening carefully when you're discussing with someone. Make sure to include all the aspects in your process of learning. It is said in the Upanishads:

'Vada-vada jayate tatvabodha.'

(Debate and discussion enhance your knowledge and understanding.)

Learn to respect others' opinions and thoughts. Be a keen learner and welcome all the knowledge coming towards you with utter eagerness.

Do you think that the various parts of general knowledge or GK are different and you should study them separately? Well, you are not alone.

But it's not a very good idea. Try to connect them. They are mostly interconnected. It would widen your vision and understanding.

Also, your study materials should be organised. Don't look for unlimited resources for a single topic. It may confuse you. At the same time, make sure your resources are diverse, and don't forget to makes notes.

To be very frank, superficial knowledge cannot take you places. It's not difficult to judge the level of your knowledge and understanding from your written answers. Our answers/ expressions should reflect maturity. For that, **we need to go deeper and grasp the essence of topics**.

6

Why becoming tech-savvy is so important

Remember setting up the antenna, moving and turning it to check if your television set is getting a signal? If you're a '90s kid, you would. If you are younger, then you missed the fun!

When television sets started to find a place inside middle-class households, it stirred the nation. Who would have thought that you could get a whole world of entertainment into a box set, watching *Chitrahaar*, *Spiderman*, *Shaktimaan* or the Sunday 4 p.m. movie! That was the era of togetherness when neighbours who didn't have a TV would gather at one house to watch *Ramayan* or *Mahabharat*.

It was unbelievable, really. It was not just about the technology; people were also concerned about the effect, mostly adverse, on the younger generation. They thought that television was going to ruin the new generation. The same thought hit us when mobile phones became the new normal post 2000.

Mobile and internet are part of the biggest revolution of this era. Just one click and Google comes up with millions of answers. Wikipedia has turned into the greatest online encyclopaedia. Then came mainstream media, followed by the exciting world of social media where you don't need the approval of an editor to share your thoughts or stories. Social media brought a sense of freedom—the freedom of expression. It became an open platform to share your thoughts and discuss social/political matters freely, irrespective of class or creed.

Now that you are quite familiar with this gift of technology, the different models of mobiles in your hands and an entire world of internet a click away, innumerable channels and OTT platforms on your TV, can you even imagine a life without the mobile or the internet? Those orthodox people who were worried about the adverse effects of TV, mobile or the internet are now the regular consumers of technology. Let's be honest and accept that life without technology is unimaginable.

So, if we can use technology in our daily life—for entertainment or to connect with people—why hesitate using it for learning and building knowledge? If we talk about the Civil Services or any other competitive exams, the internet is a great medium to learn and expand our knowledge base. It's somewhat like Darwin's theory of '**survival of the fittest**'. Time is changing rapidly, and we must learn to keep pace with time.

An anonymous poet has written:

'Iss masheeni daur mein raftaar hi pehchaan hain,
Dheere dheere jo chaloge, gumshuda ho jaaoge.'

(In this rapidly moving world, your pace is your identity. If you don't match your pace with the world, you will be lost.)

Now, understand that the nature of the Civil Service examination is diverse and dynamic. It's essential to follow a number of resources to stay updated. Apart from books and newspapers, sensible usage of the internet, various relevant websites and YouTube videos is significant. There are so many websites that provide relevant content. You might feel tempted to collect all the information, but make sure that you are using right and reliable websites or resources. You cannot trust the sparkle of the internet blindly.

The internet is addictive, and the youth need to understand that excess and unwise usage of the internet can be harmful. Invention of the internet is a boon but once you get addicted, it can mess with your sense of time. The content you keep reading can put psychological pressure and may affect you negatively. A bulk of the young generation has left themselves wandering in the abyss of this addiction of Facebook or WhatsApp. So balance, my friend, is crucial. Keep your sense and sensibility intact while using the internet. Don't get carried away and become addicted.

7

Say no to perfection

Edmond Mbiaka has said, 'Perfection is a goal that will forever remain impossible for any human being to achieve. Therefore, the only achievable goal is to strive to become the best that you can possibly be.'

It is also mentioned in Article 51A(j) of the Constitution of India—'**to strive towards excellence in all spheres of individual and collective activity so that the nation constantly rises to higher levels of endeavour and achievement**'.

Everybody should make efforts to progress in their personal and social lives. We must leave no stone unturned to accomplish what we aim for.

If we look around, we would realise that everybody wants to make a mark and is trying their best to do better and to be a better version of themselves. A farmer, as he reaps the crops of his hard work, plans to introduce new technique and work even harder so that the next time his crops flourish even more. A businessman dreams of getting more and more customers so that his balance sheet shows more profit. A lad struggling with a nine-to-five job keeps his fingers crossed for an appraisal or a promotion. Similarly, a student hopes and tries to climb the various steps of competitive examinations and finally embraces the dream he/she has been nurturing for a long time.

The desire to improve is natural. It actually leads you in a relevant direction. It reminds me of **Ralph Waldo Emerson**'s quote dedicated to the youth. He says:

'Brave men who work while others sleep,
Who dare while others fly…
They build a nation's pillars deep
And lift them to the sky.'

Our passion and our dedication to achieve success is one thing, but an obsession to achieve something is a different thing altogether. In the course of preparation, some students get obsessed with success, and begin to act like a perfectionist, or rather, a superhuman. They forget that perfection is a myth and you don't really need to be perfect to achieve success.

In fact, it's unfair to seek perfection. We'd end up being too hard on ourselves. There's an old saying, '**There's no perfect way. There are many good ways**.'

We are not superhumans. Honestly, we don't need to be. The successful people around the world are not superheroes, are they? We just need **determination, consistency and a positive attitude**. One more thing: We must try to grow every day, to be a better version of ourselves following what someone said, '**I am better than I was yesterday, but not as good as I will be tomorrow**.'

Have you ever met someone who is an expert in planning but incapable of achieving his/her goals? Ever thought what could be the reason behind their unsuccessful attempts? It's because their goals are not in sync with the ground reality. Setting goals is a good idea, yes. However, setting unrealistic goals is impractical.

Some students seek perfection in whatever they do. They want everything to be spot on. For example, they think that their study materials, notes, test series, the process of revision and even their daily routine should always be at their best. Only then can they achieve success and a rank to be proud of. They are so emotionally invested in the process that they make a long to-do list, plan like a tourist and create a tight schedule, but when it's time to follow the routine or check the to-do list, they start losing their enthusiasm. Result? They end up with a huge backlog and their aim, eventually, dwindles.

So the million-dollar question is: What should we do to save ourselves from this unnecessary stress and negativity? And how?

Firstly, whenever we make a study plan or routine, we should keep our habits, circumstances, capabilities, time availability and the level of our ambition in mind. Be rational and practical when you make plans rather than think you can be a superman and achieve whatever you aim for.

We should not compare ourselves with others. Everyone has their own capabilities, lifestyle, circumstances and habits. Everyone is unique in their own way. Everyone has their own style of working. We should follow our own style, something that works for us. Setting unrealistic or impossible rules or goals in order to copy others is not a good idea. Those goals and rules might work for them but maybe it's not going to work for us.

It's good to be inspired by successful people but copying them while chasing perfection can disconnect you from the actual reality.

Secondly, students read competitive books which feature several toppers, their success stories and interviews. It's natural to feel impressed. We should definitely feel inspired, but at the same time, we should not follow anyone blindly. We all have our own personalities, our own talent, our own method and we should follow them.

It's important to understand that a regular candidate and a topper are not drastically different from each other. They both are students and aspirants. It makes you feel good, right? Yes, it's true. If you read the toppers' interviews, you may notice them accepting that they were not expecting such a remarkable result. So, any sensible, determined, hardworking candidate can be a topper.

Some aspirants get confused by reading toppers' interviews, which is natural. Guess what? Every topper has a different preparation method, different circumstances and a different success story. For example, some candidates juggle full-time jobs with their preparation. Tough, right? Some candidates manage their regular academic studies and exam preparation while some drop everything else to prepare for competitive exams. So, how many success stories or preparation methods can you follow? I'd say that the best preparation is the preparation that you do according to your own capability, sensibility and circumstances.

Be practical. Set small, realistic goals and try hard to achieve them. Never stop learning and gathering knowledge. Try to improve every single day and stay stress-free.

But when we are talking about perfection, we are talking about impractical, unreasonable perfection. It doesn't mean that it's okay to take your efforts lightly. It undoubtedly requires a dedicated effort. If you are serious about your aim, try your best and try to be the best as per your capability. Be a smart, endeavouring and loyal candidate. Success or failure is a part of life but you must feel that your effort was genuine and honest, that your preparation wasn't complete. This feeling enhances the chances of your success manifold.

Most importantly, enjoy the journey. Then you would realise that sometimes the journey is more exciting and beautiful than the destination. A poet has said:

'Manzil mile ya nahi, mujhe uska gam nahin,
Manzil ki justju mein mera karwan to hai.'

(I don't care whether I reach my destination or not. I am content with the pursuit of the destination.)

F.E. Marie has rightly said, 'Even when you fall, even when nothing goes as you expected, even then, be proud of yourself. You tried, and there is nothing more courageous than trying.'

Let's remember the mantra, 'keep going', guided by the hands of our courage and determination and chase our dreams.

8

The three guiding principles of life

Everyone needs guidance and motivation in life, no matter what they do. Genuine, careful guidance enlightens our path and makes our journey a little easier. I particularly connect with three guiding principles from Indian philosophy that help us reach the zenith of success. I strongly believe in their power and I'd like to tell you that these guiding principles have played pivotal roles in my success too.

The first principle is **Nishkama Karma** from the Gita.

'Karmanye vadhikaraste, ma phaleshu kadachan.
Ma karm phala heturbhu, ma te sangotsav karmani.'

(On your duty only you have right. Not on the fruits of it ever. Never for the desire for fruit should you perform. Never should you be attracted to inaction [in performance of your duties].)

In other words, it means: **Keep working without expecting positive results. Believe in your actions, perform your duties and success will follow**.

Difficult, isn't it, to keep working hard without any expectations?

Moreover, if there's no expectation and no hope for results, then why would you want to work, right? In this case, where would you draw motivation from?

As per my insight and understanding, nishkama karma or working without expectations/attachment doesn't stop you from hoping for positive results. It actually inspires you to work hard for better results, without being too attached to results.

Okay, let's accept it. There's a certain charm in basking in the glory of prospective results. But at the same time, there's a drawback. If you keep thinking about the results, you fail to enjoy the lessons you learn during the work or process of preparation. Thus, it is important to stay calm, strong and stable while you are progressing towards your destination. Here comes the theory of working without expecting the fruits of your actions: **You can't control the results but you can certainly control your own attitude**.

Makes sense, right?

The second guiding principle is from Jainism—**Anekantavada (non-absoluteness)**. It broadly means 'respecting others' views'. This unique doctrine tells us that truth is manifold. It has various versions from various perspectives. It's about peoples' perspectives, and no perspective is completely right or wrong.

Remember the story of an elephant and seven blind men? Seven blind men found an elephant standing on a road. Since they could not see the animal, they touched it and started conceptualising and describing it. They were touching different parts of the animal, so obviously their descriptions were different from each other. To the man who touched its ear, the animal felt like a fan. To the man who touched its tail, the elephant felt like a broom. To the man who touched its leg, the animal felt like a pillar. They all might be wrong in each other's mind, but they were right from their own perspective. So, something that is right for you can be wrong for others. That doesn't necessarily make you wrong or the others right.

So, the theory of *anekantavada* or many-sidedness teaches us to understand and respect someone else's perspective. Do not blatantly reject someone else's perspective just because you do not agree with them. In case you are such a person who doesn't try to understand other people's perspective, you could end up being labelled as a difficult or an insensitive person.

So, let's take a quick test to see if you are a difficult person or not. I found an interesting post on social media:

Who is a difficult person?

1. If you think everyone is wrong and you are always right, then you are turning into a difficult person.
2. You can be a difficult person if you always manage to find something negative about every person or thing.

3. If you are perpetually unimpressed, beware, you are on the way to becoming a difficult person.
4. You are a difficult person if you argue about every little thing just for the heck of it.
5. Are you always bothered about others, like what are they doing? Why are they doing that? What could be the possible reason for their actions or behaviour? Or do you pretend to be a mind reader and think that you know everything? Yes? So, are you the Almighty? Certainly not. You are a difficult person.
6. Ever felt that people avoid you? Wondered why? Maybe you have the traits of a difficult person.
7. If you have readymade suggestions for others but not one for yourself, as you feel that you don't need to improve, you are a difficult person.
8. If you are too egoistic to say 'I'm sorry', you are a difficult person.
9. If you have the tendency to keep grudges for a long period, if you are too proud to forgive others, you are a difficult person.
10. If you're unable to digest gossip, you are a difficult person.

Difficult people need to be sensible and sensitive, they need to compose their mind, or else they may find themselves walking alone on a deserted path.

So, don't be one if you want to be a happy, social person. Learn to accept other people's views.

Anekantavada teaches acceptance. Acceptance can be a solution to many problems. Let's try to understand it this way:

Acceptance

When we don't accept an undesired event, it becomes **anger**.

When we accept it, it becomes **tolerance**.

When we don't accept uncertainty, it becomes **fear**.

When we accept it, it becomes an **adventure**.

When we don't accept others' bad behaviour towards us, it becomes **hatred**.

When we accept it, it becomes **forgiveness**.

When we don't accept someone else's success, it becomes **jealousy**.

When we accept it, it becomes **inspiration**.

Not just in life, *anekantavada* helps and guides us during our exam preparation as well. In written tests and interviews, many-sidedness acts as an elixir. It reflects maturity and positivity when we answer, whether it's a written test or oral, without being an extremist. When we become a little flexible and learn to respect others' opinions, it promotes tolerance and makes our journey a tad easier.

My third favourite guiding principle is **Madhyam Marga (the middle path)**.

Gautam Buddha suggested to ignore extremes and follow the middle path. There's an old saying: **excess of everything is bad**.

The middle path helps you reconcile. It helps you find a friendly path to settle an argument.

During examination preparation, the middle path helps you build an integrated approach and a balanced view. Balance, my friend, is crucial. It makes your journey smoother. You might be wondering how you could use this principle in your life. I'll tell you about the use of simple yet relevant words, neither too easy nor too difficult. Your answers shouldn't be too long nor too short.

So these are the three guiding principles of my life. I would suggest you to you follow these principles as well and then you can write the story of a better and brighter future.

9

Why the middle path is the golden path

Have you ever thought why we aspire to appear in the Civil Services exam or any other competitive exam? Why do we work so hard, so ardently, to crack these exams? Why do we refuse to be affected by pressure and stress, and keep going on devotedly on a path full of hurdles to achieve what we have aimed for?

It's true that everybody has their own goals and priorities, but if we analyse closely, some common things would come to our mind as the answer:

- A desire to have a better future and a happy life
- An effort to be the best version of ourselves
- The quest for a good and prestigious career
- The need to fulfil the expectations of our parents and teachers
- The wish to make our dreams come true

Chasing our dreams and giving them a definite and desired contour is not that difficult, trust me, but it's not that easy either. Success does not move on a linear path. Preparing for the Civil Services exam is like dealing with life—a winding road, full of ups and downs, even straight and smooth at times. Just the way life is vast and multifunctional, the Civil Services preparation is also lengthy and twisted. In my personal opinion, following the middle path is a glorious way to overcome this burden, dilemma and stress.

The middle path or golden mean, one of the most insightful philosophies of Buddhism, is also known as *majjhima patipada* in Pali literature. Buddha has suggested that we should avoid both absolute abstinence and overindulgence. And here comes the theory of the golden mean. This philosophy is close to the process of inclusiveness and endurance in the Upanishads.

Buddha's middle path is very close to Mahavira's philosophy of *anekantavada*. It tells us that no assertion is absolute. Everything has its own perspective. If we try, we can see things in a different light and we may get enlightened. Remember the story of the elephant and seven blind men? Even truth has many faces. Everybody has their own truths. Your truth can be a lie in someone else's opinion. There's an old saying, '**The truth lies somewhere in the middle**.'

Sometimes truth is relative, according to the time frame, country, society or even circumstances. For example, the criterion for morality in our country is quite different from the West. In some countries, capital punishment is illegal as they believe it's a breach of human rights, while certain countries find it justified. In some countries, homosexuality or same sex marriage is perfectly okay but some find it illegal and unnatural. So there are several examples to understand this concept. It's all about perspective or mentality.

So now that our concept is clear, let's discuss how these two significant philosophies can make our life and the process of preparation for examinations less stressful.

- Have you ever felt confused while writing an essay, as though your thoughts were jumbled—what to write, what to skip? The golden mean theory can help you sort your thoughts out.
- You can't write a good essay until you cover all the possible aspects of the subject, including the pros and cons. Many-sidedness and the golden mean can be really helpful in organising your thoughts.
- While preparing for exams, your learner's attitude can be an asset. For that, you need to be an advocate of the middle path, instead of being drawn towards the extremes. The middle path teaches you to respect others' opinions.
- Many times, while explaining certain topics in the written papers or even interviews, you need to express your views or opinions. Your balanced view that comes after a thorough analysis of the pros and cons gets highly appreciated. You cannot get this if you are rigid in expressing your views.
- The process of preparation can be tiring, even boring at times. It's easy to give up, but difficult to carry on

without being deterred. Even life gets boring, stressful and unfair at times, no? It's natural. The philosophy of many-sidedness, the golden path and nishkama karma (working hard without any expectations) help you deal with such tough situations. So, being a dedicated student without attachment to results is a rather essential ingredient in the preparation of the Civil Services exam and for other exams as well.

- If you think too much about perfection, it turns into an obsession. But when you try and understand the gist of many-sidedness, that nothing is best, or everything has its own perspective, you are able to prepare in a more relaxed way.
- The interview is a crucial stage, don't you agree? What's important when you're sitting in an interview room? Your politeness and spontaneity make a big difference. Have you ever thought why some people are so polite? Because they understand that knowledge is limitless and they respect peoples' opinions. They cannot be Mr Know-it-all. This feeling makes you realise that you are nothing in front of the vastness of knowledge. It reminds me of an insightful quote: '**Knowledge is a progressive discovery of our own ignorance**.'

The good thing is, these principles are not just relevant for some exam but they also guide you at various stages of life. They make you more mature, tolerant, strong, polite and capable. You just need to understand this and gradually instil these values in your life.

10

Never, never, never give up

Benjamin Franklin rightly said, '**Out of adversity comes opportunity**.'

Let's understand this quote through the famous 'success iceberg'.

You must have heard of the famous scientist Thomas Edison who invented the light bulb after failing numerous times. It was his dedication, patience and determination that had illuminated the light bulb. You know what he said about the failures? He said, '**I have not failed. I've just found ten thousand ways that won't work**.'

This is what you call a positive attitude. An attitude where no failure can deter you from trying and learning.

Strangely, sometimes we give up or feel too tired to try when we are about to achieve success. Edison has rightly said, '**Many of life's failures** are people who did not **realise how close they** were to success when **they** gave up.'

Now let me share some inspirational, real-life success stories that will help you understand the power of 'not giving up'.

Beno Zephine

Beno Zephine was a soft-spoken, blind woman who worked at the State Bank of India (SBI) as a probationary officer

(PO). She had been an active student since her childhood and always used to participate in debate competitions. Her dreams changed their direction and she started preparing for the Civil Service examination. Unfortunately, the resources in Braille were very limited. But Beno never allowed her disability to come between her and success, and eventually, she got selected. Today Beno is an Indian diplomat, and she is the first hundred per cent visually challenged Indian Foreign Service officer. She gives the credit to her parents and friends who read out books to her for hours without getting tired or annoyed.

Raja Ganpati Ramasamy

Raja completed his MBBS but wanted to be an IAS officer. So he went to Chennai to prepare for the Civil Service examination. Whenever he felt sad or troubled, his father's face flashed in front of his eyes. His father was a big support, travelling with Raja when he decided to shift to a big city. He believed his son would crack the Civil Services in his first attempt.

But Raja failed. 'Maybe I was not that focused while preparing. I need to work harder,' he thought. He started preparing with reinvigorated zest, but a sense of frustration was building somewhere in his mind. Reason? Expectations. It's difficult to carry the weight of expectations, you know. His friends were settled by then and relatives had started asking questions. His father ignored them, as he had faith that Raja would definitely succeed on the second attempt.

But luck was not on Raja's side. When he was getting ready for the second attempt, the Civil Services exam introduced the Civil Services Aptitude Test (CSAT). Raja was not very good at mathematics, and this format generated a kind of phobia and he couldn't crack it.

Now the situation was grave. He didn't have a job and he couldn't ask his parents for money. He started writing for a competitive magazine. By then, his relatives were almost hounding him to get married. One day, his mother, literally tearing up, asked him to leave this passion and get a job. It was heartbreaking, but Raja couldn't bring himself to compromise with his dream to become an IAS officer. He took up a private teaching job. The earning was decent. A little relaxed, he engrossed himself in the preparation. The third attempt brought failure, yet again, along with dark clouds of disappointment. The good thing was that he kept his dreams and passion alive. He was almost sure that the fourth attempt was going to bear fruit for him. But it didn't happen this time as well. What went wrong?

It almost broke him when his father broke down in tears in front of him. For the first time, Raja's biggest support looked hopeless. But then something flashed, a ray of hope, diminishing the gloomy hopelessness. Raja aced the State Public Service Commission (PSC) exam, with a rank of 15.

With renewed energy, he used this platform as a pillar of strength for his fifth attempt. He just couldn't let it go. His luck couldn't be that bad. Hard work pays, after all. He cracked it finally. Prelims, mains and interview, he qualified all the three phases. He did it! In this journey, his elder brother acted as a motivational force.

It was 2014. Raja got through the Uttar Pradesh cadre in the IAS. He calls his journey 'a story of failures', and his message to every aspiring candidate is, 'Never, never, never give up!'

Ghanshyam Meena

Ghanshyam hails from Jaipur and he was an engineering graduate who wanted to be a civil servant. He tried for both the state PSC exam and the UPSC exam. Fortunately, he got selected as an officer in the State Tax department in Rajasthan. In his first UPSC attempt, he couldn't qualify in the preliminary exams. In the second attempt, he qualified for the mains. He was eagerly waiting for the results but it didn't bring any joy. He failed in Hindi, a compulsory subject. Every evening, he would shrug off the tiredness of a full-time job and sit down to study. He got an interview call on his third attempt, but could go only till there. But his unsuccessful attempts could not kill his dreams. In 2015, on his fourth attempt, he eventually got selected as an IAS officer in the Bihar cadre.

Ghanshyam believes that being grounded and eternally optimistic is the secret of his success.

Sachin Kumar Vaish

An ordinary struggle can lead to extraordinary achievements. Sachin's struggles and achievements prove it. Sachin comes from Pratapgarh, Uttar Pradesh. He cracked the Civil Services exam in 2014, ranking 94. Sachin's father never compromised with his education despite financial and social problems. He couldn't afford IIT–JEE coaching, so he got himself enrolled at the State Entrance Uttar Pradesh Technical University (UPTU) through the state entrance exam.

Luck was adamant on testing his patience for a very long time. He couldn't succeed in the Special Class Railway Apprentice (SCRA) exam of the UPSC and a single mistake snatched his opportunity to clear the Graduate Aptitude Test in Engineering (GATE) examination. He didn't give up, and continued his preparation with public administration as his optional paper. Sachin cracked the Civil Services examination in his first attempt. It was his dedicated practice and revision that helped him achieve this. Can you guess how old he was when he tasted this success? Just twenty-two years and ten months. Fascinating, isn't it?

Similar to all the above stories, there's another—the story of Nishant Jain. Yeah, that's me! In my story, like every other you've read till now, one element in particular worked wonders. Have you noticed that common element? It's persistence!

The Civil Services exam is full of uncertainty. There are numerous examples (like the success stories I've shared here and also at the end of this book) where some students reached the interview stage and got rejected, while many others couldn't even qualify the preliminary or mains. But one thing is remarkably noticeable—**every successful candidate has a history of failure**.

So, naturally, we get to learn certain insightful things. What did we learn? Let's discuss.

The most prominent mantra for success is **persistence**. It keeps us going and it's a reflection of our hope. As I have mentioned earlier, several competitive exams have kept the persistence quotient as a testing meter.

Many people look enthusiastic and full of energy in the beginning but start losing their vibrancy slowly. They get tired or lazy. Sometimes, even hopeless. They start wasting time in useless activities, maybe to avoid the feeling of despair. So it's good to plan to set goals and a strict routine, but we must learn to work hard and keep our enthusiasm alive. Never forget the mantra of persistence. **Consistency**, my friend, is the key.

There's another problem that you may find in some of your friends. Overexpectation. The Civil Services require a great deal of effort and it's full of uncertainty and surprises. There's no guarantee and it's quite possible that you meet with an unexpected jolt of failure.

Sometimes failures teach us more than success. I have no hesitation in admitting, and I'm saying this from my personal experience, that I have learnt the most from one failure of life (when I couldn't clear the prelims of the Civil Service examination in my first attempt) than all my achievements and experiences.

Stagnant water rots. Similarly, a stagnant life gets tired easily. Whether we reach our destination or not, life never stops, and you should not either. **The wheel of time keeps rolling despite all the successes or failures**.

That's why I say, when it comes to our career, always keep an option ready. Some people even leave their jobs or take leave to prepare for the Civil Service examination. Some people handle their jobs and preparation at the same time (and some aspirants do incredibly well—remember the success stories?). Some students decide to get employed after finishing their studies and engross themselves in the preparation.

When you find a career option for yourself, whether it is in the public sector or private, you feel relieved and it helps you go ahead with less stress. You might have noticed in my story or in any of the stories mentioned above that some kind of employment has made our journey a little easier.

Many a time, I've observed people give up and abandon the journey when they are about to reach their destination. Despair grips them so tight that they leave the hands of hope and determination. There's a famous quote by **Thomas Edison**: 'Many of life's failures are people who did not realise how close they were to success when they gave up.'

There's something common in the above stories and I find it so appealing: this immense desire to keep moving and reach the zenith of success. It is even mentioned in the Upanishads:

'Kurvanneveha karmani jijiviset satam samah.'

(You should keep working hard if you wish to live a long and better life.)

There's something common in every successful person—the desire to make progress. It is the desire to make progress that has kept successful candidates' motivation level and self-esteem intact.

Always remember that it's not only the moment of failure when you will seek motivation. You will need it at various stages of preparation as well—moments when you will begin to doubt your abilities, moments when you will squirm under pressure. It's going to be your constant friend, a friend that brings solace. Create a pleasant and positive environment around you. Try to ignore negativity. Learn to shrug the frustration off. Let's not forget the famous quote, which is also the title of a play by the great William Shakespeare: 'All is well that ends well.'

Hurdles are inevitable. They are like a fire that doesn't spare anyone. Some burn in despair, while some rise and emerge from it like a phoenix.

If failure blocks our way, accept it gracefully. Learn from it, smile and move ahead. It reminds me of a beautiful poem by Vijay Dev Narayan Sahi. I am sharing its English translation:

When you feel broken
By the strokes of misfortune,
Weep, my dearest
It's not a shame

Several mountains weep
Inside the closed doors
Even plateaus seek
Room for their solitude

A hundred suns are melting
Behind the darkness
Not every tear is the reflection of
Cowardice.

There's another striking feature of successful candidates. They don't allow the lack of resources, disability or any other weakness to overwhelm them. They handle failure in a dignified manner so that they can carry success elegantly. Those who refuse to panic when failure strikes are the ones who carry success gracefully for a long time.

Don't take your failure or even success personally. Just make sure you make progress and greet new dreams wholeheartedly. Every day try to be a better version of yourself. Never let pessimism shroud your mind. Success can't refuse to come to you.

Never deviate from the path that may lead you to succees. Have you heard that popular and inspirational song from the Bollywood movie *Imtihaan*?

'*Ruk jaana nahin tu kahi haar ke*
Kaaton pe chal ke milenge saaye bahar ke.'

(Don't let hurdles defeat you. Walking on the thorns leads you to the blooming spring.)

11

Do you have a Plan B?

Life is a constant, enlightening journey and it never rests. It's good to keep moving. Being stagnant is not a good idea. Even water needs to flow to stay fresh and sparkling.

Everybody wants to achieve success in life to do something substantial, to create his/her own identity. It's a wonderful thing. Youngsters are particularly enthusiastic about achieving their goals. They want to achieve success and soak in its warmth as long as they can.

What is success? There's no perfect, unanimously accepted definition. But we can say we're successful if we have a respectable and satisfying livelihood; if we are happy with our personal, professional and social life. It's even better if we manage to earn respect and praise through our work and behaviour. If we are healthy, have a peaceful personal life and state of mind, then no one is more successful or happier than us. Health and peace are two beautiful aspects of happiness.

Here, Maslow's theory of hierarchy of needs comes to my mind. This interesting pyramid includes five human needs:

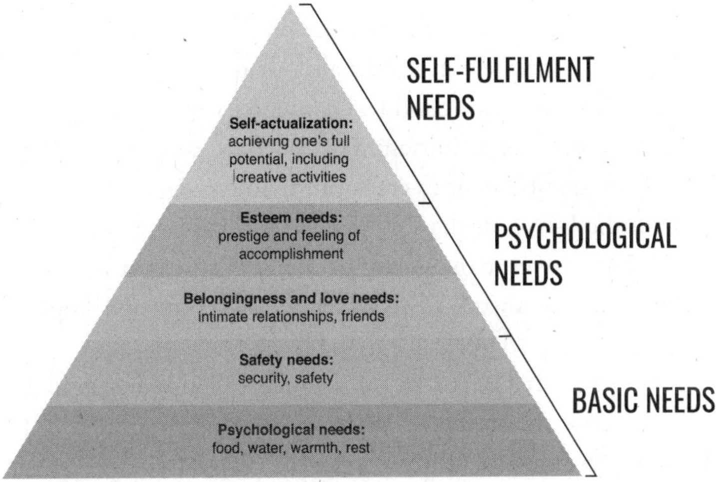

Basic needs are bodily requirements like hunger and thirst. Then comes the need for safety and security so that we can be prepared to fight our fears. Number three, very important needs: love, attachment and togetherness. A good relationship fulfils these emotional needs.

A sense of self-respect and significance or relevance of your existence—they cannot lag behind and hence, are the fourth level of needs. Last but not the least is the spiritual need of self-realisation.

It's quite difficult to fulfil all these needs. But it could be considered an ideal situation even if we achieve the first four of them. Actually, one can live a decent life with the first three too.

The good thing is that we don't need any specific designation or qualification to fulfil these needs. Anybody—an employee in the private or the public sector, a farmer or a lawyer, a teacher or a journalist—can fulfil their human needs. We often do it and feel contented. The term 'success' is very broad. Its definition may vary from person to person.

Who doesn't want to crack prestigious competitive exams (be it the UPSC or the IIT–JEE/NEET/CAT/CLAT/NET–JRF)? You meet many young people. I'm sure you have seen the dream of success in competitive exams in the hopeful eyes of young students.

It's true that there are so many career options, but the Civil Services stands out. There's something charming about them. And despite all the challenges, it continues to be the top draw among aspirants. In fact, the fascination to ace Civil Services exam has grown. Initially, the candidates were mostly from Uttar Pradesh and Bihar, but now students from every part of India, be it the North-east, Jammu & Kashmir, Tamil Nadu or Rajasthan, are trying their luck.

There's something magnetic about the Indian Civil Services. It attracts the youth of every class, creed, region or language. Why is it so popular? We all know that the field of IAS/IPS is vast. Its sphere of functions is wide and diverse. This field gives an opportunity to connect with people directly and it's extremely inspiring to realise that in this field, you have tremendous scope of contributing to the society and the country. I think these are some reasons why Civil Services find a special place in the aspirations of the youth.

A number of young students leave their hometowns and move to bigger cities like Delhi, Chennai, Patna, Bengaluru, Jaipur, Indore and Hyderabad with the passion of becoming an IAS officer. But of course everyone cannot afford to move to the metros, so they continue preparing in their hometowns. I have noticed these days many candidates succeed without joining coaching classes, which was kind of a craze some years back. Actually, the internet has become their coaching class. With so much study material and resources available online, it definitely helps if we are smart enough to use them properly.

Further, the length of the UPSC journey also varies for different candidates. Some students take two years to crack the exams while some make it a five-year plan.

I have observed that middle-class students or those who come from weak financial backgrounds have this pressure to perform well all the time. They constantly battle this pressure and dilemma, like 'What if I don't get selected?' or 'What would I do after that? How would I face my family? What about their expectations?' Some aspirants are so passionate, or let me say 'obsessed', that they think that their life would be useless if they don't become an IAS officer; like that would be the end of the road. That leads to uncalled-for depression.

Why do they think like that? Remember we spoke about career options and employability? That's the reason. Their minds run in a straight line. They don't think about any other career option or their employability.

Now we know the significance of keeping a career option and understanding your employability. Although I strongly believe that it's crucial to be determined and hardworking, all the same, having a respectable career option can save us from unnecessary pressure. It may certainly help us prepare with a stress-free mind.

You would find yourself a little relaxed thinking that even if the UPSC doesn't work out, you have something else to look forward to. You'd feel a sense of relief.

However, it's not essential to keep an alternate career option. There are a number of successful candidates who just focused on Civil Services as their only career option. But we all have different levels of mental strength. How can anyone concentrate on studies if they are constantly worried about something they can't control? Life goes on. It never rests. It wouldn't wait for you. So it's a good idea to keep a career option so that you can prepare with a relaxed mind, so that you can keep up with life.

You might be wondering about the options. What could they be? What can you do to support yourself financially in case you take longer than expected?

This is the '**back-up plan**'. There's a famous idiom: "**Don't put all your eggs in one basket**." It means, do not depend on one thing or a single plan of action. So, what could be your back-up plan? First and foremost, you should choose things as per your interests or aptitude. I'm sharing some important options.

1. **Other examinations conducted by UPSC:**

   Other than the Civil Services exam, UPSC conducts some other exams also. The aspirants can appear in the following exams, conducted by the UPSC every year, according to their aptitude and eligibility.

   a) Indian Forest Service Examination
   b) Engineering Services Examination
   c) Indian Economic Service and Indian Statistical Service Examination
   d) Combined Medical Services Examination
   e) Central Armed Police Forces Examination

   All the above examinations are for recruitment of Group A posts of the Central Civil Services, Government of India. These services may provide challenging and prestigious career options.

2. **Examinations conducted by the State Public Service Commissions:**

   The Public Service Commissions of Indian states conducts exams for Group A and Group B (both gazetted and non-gazetted) posts. Apart from these, there are many other vacancies for which exams are conducted by state PSCs. I think any aspirant who is preparing for UPSC can easily prepare for state Civil Service examination. Almost every state has a paper for their official language.

3. **Other various competitive examinations:** Apart from the PSC examinations, several boards/ commissions of central and state governments conduct competitive exams for various posts.
   a) Parliament of India, Joint Recruitment Cell (JRC)
   b) SSC (Staff Selection Commission's Combined Graduate Level exam)
   c) Delhi Subordinate Services Selection Board (DSSSB)
   d) Railway Recruitment Boards (RRBs)
   e) The Institute of Banking Personnel Selection (IBPS), etc.

   The aforementioned competitive examinations can provide options for respectable careers. How do you prepare for these? They usually set questions from four main subjects—general knowledge, English, reasoning and arithmetic—that somehow match with UPSC–CSAT.

4. **Other career opportunities**: If you are planning a back-up career while preparing, here are some other attractive options.
   a) NET–JRF (teaching and research): It's a very prestigious career. After clearing NET, you can apply for the post of assistant professor at any college or university. If you qualify for JRF, you get fellowship for research (MPhil/PhD).
   b) Media and mass communication

c) Advertising and public relations
d) Radio or television
e) Translation and creative writing
f) You can turn into an entrepreneur and start your own business. It's, in fact, a great idea, for you can employ other people and contribute to the development of society and nation.
g) A newly evolved career option is social work. You can join an NGO and work part-time. It can help you earn money and experience as well. Plus you'll be contributing to the betterment of the society. Many candidates join NGOs before the interview just to gain some social work experience.
h) Diploma/post-graduation/research or higher studies: Some aspirants continue their higher studies, through distance education, while preparing or waiting for the interview.

   There are three benefits of doing this. First, you create a profile for the period when you were not really gainfully employed. Second, these studies can be helpful for your optional subject or general studies. Third, when you have a good degree, you feel more confident and it enhances your employability as well. I had done a Post Graduate Diploma in Translation (PGDT) from IGNOU and it helped me get a job in the Parliament of India.

But remember, and remember this clearly, that don't overthink about these options. They are supposed to make things easier for you and not confusing. Don't get distracted from your aim. I have shared these career options just to tell you that there's a world beyond the stars. Your life won't stop in case you don't succeed in the Civil Service examination, and these options would help you move on. Moving on is one of the most difficult but important things you can learn in life. Follow the mantra of moving on and go ahead.

'**Your life is your message to the world, make sure it's inspiring.**'

– *Anonymous*

12
New beginning, new resolutions

I'll tell you a story.

There was pin drop silence in a class as students looked curiously at the blackboard. It was blank, well, almost, except for a line. '**Can you make this line smaller?**' the teacher asked, a soft smile playing on his lips.

Several students tried, as though it was an easy task. They picked the duster and wiped off part of the line. Easy, no? It was, actually. But the teacher didn't mean to ask a very simple question. One quiet student finally impressed him. What did he do? He didn't even use the duster. He picked up a tiny piece of chalk and simply drew a longer line beside that line. Naturally, the previous line became smaller without even being touched.

The teacher was trying to convey an important message. '**We don't rise by dragging other people down. We rise by lifting ourselves up**.' We small-town struggling students quite relate to it. So when we try to grow and rise, we should keep in mind that we don't have to diminish someone else's talent. We just need to polish our own. This policy of lifting ourselves could be a good start to the process of transforming our lives.

Every morning is another chance for a new start. Not just every morning; every new week, month and every new year arrives with new hope, dreams and energy to start afresh. Every new year starts with a spate of resolutions. How many people manage to keep these resolutions is a different question altogether.

On a serious note, resolutions help you set goals. We make resolutions to get rid of bad habits or to embrace new ones. We don't want to lag behind, do we?

When we make resolutions, we feel like it's going to be a new start. We feel determined to keep all the promises we make to ourselves. Resolutions evoke hope and a sense of renewal. It seems it would abolish everything bad and fill our life with new energy, success and happiness.

Do you make resolutions? Have you ever thought of it like a progress report? How many resolutions did you keep and how many of them were forgotten? The railway ministry announces new trains every year, exciting the masses. But what about old trains? The management of timings and routes of old trains is equally important. Similarly, making new resolutions is fine but keeping the old ones is also important.

Whether you keep your resolutions or forget them, the enthusiasm of new year resolutions remains the same. It's natural and it shows your will to amend and adapt to life.

I have been making new year resolutions and I'll make a resolution list this time too. Certain things change, of course. They are our needs and priorities.

Let's make ten inspiring resolutions. Interestingly, they are not very difficult to apply. So, why wait for new year's? Let's create a wishlist and embrace some resolutions with the new morning.

1. Make continuity and **consistency** a part of your life. When you adopt a new habit, make sure it sustains.
2. Smile. That soft **smile** playing on your lips makes you look pleasant and positive, and it helps you fight your troubles.
3. Seize the day. Feel blessed if it's a joyful day and enjoy it wholeheartedly. Don't postpone it for some other time. Learn from the past and keep moving towards the future.
4. Set small and realistic goals. It's so exciting to check goals off your list. Savour the sense of achievement even if it's a small one. Don't forget to celebrate these little moments of happiness.
5. Learn to **respect other people's views** and opinions. The philosophy of many-sidedness instils patience and endurance and makes you a more mature person.

Don't be rigid about your own views; follow the middle path.

6. **Work hard,** but don't be too worried about the results. Too much attachment to the future can act as a distraction. Believe in action without the desire of results. It's going to be fruitful, eventually. Unexpected positive results are so exciting!
7. Make new friends but don't forget old ones. There may be innumerable troubles in life but you can overcome them if you nurture and value your relationships, as they are the real asset. **Togetherness** is a blessing. Spend quality time with your dear ones.
8. Develop the tendency of helping each other.
9. **Help the needy** if you can. The smile on their lips and gratitude in their eyes will make you feel good and content. The joy of giving is priceless. How can you help others? What may seem small to you can make a big difference to someone else's life. For example, teach a poor child. Your 'small' gesture can change lives.
10. Do not ignore activities which fascinate you or **hobbies** you wish to pursue. Live them. Life is beautiful. Learn to love your life. Never hesitate to learn new things. Embrace great thoughts.

However, you can't develop these habits overnight. You'll have to practise and keep practising until they become a habit. If we accept these resolutions wholeheartedly and include them in our daily life, we become more energetic and less stressed. Optimism can help us achieve this. I am sharing a poem that I wrote in my college days:

Positive Thinking

I carry
optimism and enthusiasm
in my merry heart,
Armed with these weapons,
I believe
I'm going to win every war.

Dilemmas, doubts and despair …
I will let them go
Hurdles can try to hit me
I promise to beat them
With a beatific smile.

I'll fill my soul
With unending energy
I'll stand tall, I'll fight
I'll take the world
In my stride.
I pledge to create.

The destination is calling,
I'll brace myself

With hope and determination
To greet it, embrace it.

There is a gloominess everywhere
As though the nation is sleeping
May my message resonate
Loud and clear
Awakening and enlightening this land.

13

My journey through struggles and dreams

'And, when you want something, all the universe conspires in helping you to achieve it.'

This quote from Paulo Coelho's book, *The Alchemist*, describes the journey of my struggle and the story of my success quite aptly.

I was born and raised in Meerut, at a middle-class home in an ordinary lane.

My father worked at a private company and lived a happy, content life. Whatever he earned was enough for us. My mother supported him in everything. She has been a wonderful homemaker. She, like many Indian middle-class mothers, knew how to run the home with limited resources.

Papa had to leave studies after school but Maa was a graduate, so education naturally found a very significant place in our household. She made sure all her three children got a good education, no matter what.

I think I began dreaming about being an officer when I was in Class VIII or IX. It started at another old lane, in front of a PDS ration shop where we used to stand for hours under the scorching sun to buy grocery, with the shopkeeper often vanishing.

While I waited in the queue one afternoon, I started reading the yellow ration card. My eyes were fixed on the bottom of the card where the word *adhikaari* (officer) was printed. If there were any irregularities, I wondered if the officer could control or rectify them. If yes, then I would like to become an officer, I thought.

When I returned home, I shared this with my mother, as she prepared lunch for everyone. Maa smiled. But I think no one paid much attention to it, thinking it was just one of those things a child says.

But it stayed in my mind. I still remember an IAS officer, Mr Avnish Awasthi. He was District Collector/District Magistrate of Meerut.

I was very fond of reading newspapers since my school days. Every day I read news pieces that featured Mr Awanish Awasthi. His dedication, innovative ideas and initiatives for the betterment of the district fascinated me. The seeds of becoming an officer that were sown a few days ago had started to grow.

'**I want to be a Collector**,' I said to my elder brother.

He looked impressed. 'Well, you will have to clear the Civil Services exam to achieve that.'

I grew thoughtful.

'It's quite tough, you know,' he added.

Days rolled on. I completed my senior secondary from a Hindi-medium government school. Fortunately, I was the topper from my district.

While I liked studying science and commerce, I had a natural inclination towards the humanities. Thankfully, I realised it by the time I completed my 10+2. It helps a lot when you realise what you want early in your life. Those days, people tended to believe that students from the humanities stream performed better in the UPSC exams.

While many of my classmates were preparing for chartered accountancy, I, along with my two friends, decided to complete my graduation. It was financially difficult to shift to a big city like Delhi or Allahabad to pursue our education, so I stayed back and studied in Meerut. I completed my graduation with history, political science and English literature as the main subjects. Then I went on to complete my postgraduation in Hindi literature.

I have some fond memories of my college days where I was quite active in extracurricular activities. During graduation, I had participated in a number of debates, elocutions, poem recitations and essay-writing competitions and in most of the competitions, I secured the first position.

NCC and NSS were also my areas of interest. I remember how we started a door-to-door campaign during an NSS camp. We used to visit people to collect medicines that were no longer useful to them. Then we would distribute those medicines among poor people. I had been the editor of our college magazine, *Abhivyakti*. I got tremendous exposure and confidence. Although I spent a lot of time in extracurricular and social activities, I secured a place in the university merit list.

I can never forget my teachers, especially our principal Dr S.K. Agarwal and our Hindi lecturer Dr Ramayagya Maurya. Principal sir was a kind and hardworking person. Extremely positive and motivated, he could inspire with a few words. It's difficult to find such a man and teacher. I still remember how delighted he was when I got the first prize in a debate competition. He even offered us a jalebi treat! It's so special and uplifting when a teacher encourages you and genuinely feels happy for you.

When your dreams are big, hurdles are inevitable. There were certain financial constraints. My two friends and I used to work part-time after our Class X board exams. It was mostly proofreading or creative writing. These small, part-time jobs taught us big lessons.

The story of our friendship is so dramatic and filmy. We were like the '**3 idiots**' of real life. Sumit liked writing and Vatan enjoyed sketching. Reading and writing poems was my favourite way to relax. We were kind of inseparable. We did our graduation together. We did our part-time jobs together. We would just take our bicycles and roam around, discussing life, philosophy and every possible topic. More on them later.

Something really interesting happened during our postgraduation. It was a memorable incident and became the turning point of my life. There was a senior, a very kind-hearted man whom I often interacted with. One fine day, he asked a very interesting question. '**Suppose there's a dark room and you light a bulb near the floor, how much light could it provide to brighten the room? And what if you hanged that bulb on the wall? Would it make the room brighter?**'

There was a deep message hidden in this question. And I got it. If you have the capability to achieve big, dream big and try your best to achieve your dream!

I started preparing for the NET–JRF exam. Fortunately, I qualified in the exam. Another positive news came knocking. Having cleared the MPhil entrance test at Delhi University, I could finally go to Delhi and fulfil my dream.

It was the first time I stayed away from my home and family. It was difficult for me. I was a nostalgic, homesick kind of guy.

While doing my MPhil, I appeared for the UPSC Civil Services preliminary exam as well as the Uttar Pradesh State PSC prelims. My preparation was good and enthusiasm over-the-top as I always did exceptionally well in all my academic examinations. But I was not among the successful candidates. I couldn't make the cut in either of the examinations, falling short of just two–three marks. It was a painful blow as it was the first time I tasted failure in my life. It kind of shattered my strength. I thought it was the end of the road as the shadow of despair tried to engulf me. I found it difficult to carry the burden of my failure.

My career and future prospects seemed bleak. That was the time poetry and literature came to my rescue. I found shelter in books and tried to keep myself motivated with the help of some inspiring books.

It was one of the toughest phases of my life. But my family, especially my elder brother, acted as a pain-relieving balm to my agonies. The emotional support that I received from them was so uplifting.

I can say that their faith in me was much stronger than my own self-belief. It strengthened my courage. Then the result of another competitive exam (as a translator in the Parliament Secretariat) came as a breath of fresh air. I submitted my MPhil thesis and joined my job.

This job boosted my confidence and I learnt a lot. Plus, it relieved the stress of joblessness. And I feel this job security was one of the reasons I was able to concentrate on my studies, despite the demanding nature of the job.

While working, I appeared again for UPSC CSE. This time, luck was on my side. I qualified for the mains and got an interview call. My interview went on for thirty-five minutes. Interestingly, during the interview and even after that, my mind was totally calm and composed.

When you are too close to getting selected, your mind and heart work in a very different way. Every day, I eagerly waited for the result. A volley of questions whirled inside my head—'What if I don't get selected? Was my performance good enough? Is my life really going to change? Is my dream finally going to turn into a reality?' Then, I tried to calm myself. I told myself, 'You couldn't succeed in the first attempt. This time you got a call for an interview. You performed well.

Your interview was a great learning experience. Trust me, it is a big deal. You do have a respectable job. Isn't it a great relief?'

3 July 2015. It was a scorching summer afternoon when I came to know the final result of the UPSC exams was going to be announced the next day. I felt like going home and seeing the results with my family. It was a Saturday, so going home was not a problem. I boarded a bus from Anand Vihar bus stand and went home.

It was a calm afternoon when we were waiting for the results. All had gathered in the room. My heart was beating a little faster than usual but I noticed that my family members were more nervous than me. I got a call at 1 p.m. I got the rank of 13, the highest among candidates who wrote the paper in an Indian language. After that, my phone didn't stop ringing the whole day. All the congratulatory messages and encouraging words made me a little emotional. Later, we got to know that I had got the third-highest marks in the mains exam, the highest in the essay paper and also the highest in my optional subject. My total score was 1001 and to me, it was like an auspicious sign.

Success never comes alone. It brings a lot of expectations and responsibilities. One of the expectations is to carry and maintain the success. It's difficult to carry success gracefully. Many people immediately change their attitude the moment they achieve something big. They feel so happy and proud that a sense of superiority creeps into their psyche.

Success demands maturity and thoughtfulness. I feel glad and thankful that I could value and respect my success and manage to stay grounded. I cannot thank my family and friends enough.

Many felicitation ceremonies were organised and I got a number of chances to speak to enthusiastic aspirants. I feel truly humbled for all the acknowledgements but one event is closest to my heart—the felicitation ceremony at the Parliament's Balayogi Auditorium, in the presence of Lok Sabha Speaker Mrs Sumitra Mahajan.

It was a big day for me. Many esteemed people like the then Minister of State for Parliamentary Affairs and the Secretary General of Lok Sabha were also present along with all the officers and staff of the Secretariat where I had been working for the last two years.

I feel it was not just my personal honour. It was the honour of a young man and an aspirant who belonged to a middle-class background and had struggled to achieve what he had aimed for. It was an honour of every ordinary man who dared to dream big and succeeded.

Whenever I think about those golden moments, I feel things have changed. And sometimes it feels that nothing has changed. Certain things have certainly changed, like now I don't have to fill examination forms again and again. Like my family has achieved a sense of contentment, for I am settled. I have a more respectful stature in society. But certain things haven't changed and I don't want them to change—like my hunger to learn new things, to improve and to face challenges with the same determination and the passion for my work.

When someone asks about my success mantra, my high rank in the UPSC, I tell them that there were three main factors that helped me. First, my **diverse knowledge base and experience**, second, my **writing skills** and third, my **balanced view** of things.

This journey was a wonderful learning experience. Every job, every institution, every teacher and every friend has taught me a lot, and these lessons are priceless. My friends used to say, 'Your preparation was calm and silent but your success roared.'

I completed my training at Lal Bahadur Shastri National Academy of Administration, the training institute of IAS officers in Mussoorie. I made a lot of friends there. At the academy, I participated in various cultural programmes as an anchor. It was an interesting experience.

I finally got recruited into the Rajasthan cadre. I have been posted in Alwar, Kotra (Udaipur), Mount Abu, Ajmer and Jaipur so far. Kotra was the most exciting posting. Kotra is one of the most backward and interior places of Rajasthan. It's a tribal area in Udaipur district. Working at Kotra gave me an opportunity to understand tribal life very closely. During this stint, I tried my best to provide a sensible and effective administration.

There's one more thing that didn't change with time—my love for writing. Despite my tight work schedule, I have always tried to spare some time for my hobby. I have written several books. I have written a book on Civil Services preparation—*All About UPSC Civil Services Exam*. This book was very well received by aspirants and it makes me feel so glad that readers found this book helpful and inspiring. Besides that, I have compiled a book of my poems for children.

Time and experience make things happen. Things that felt like a big deal a few years ago seem quite normal now. I got several opportunities to appear on platforms like Doordarshan, BBC, All India Radio (AIR), Lok Sabha TV, Lallantop and Josh Talks as a speaker or a panelist.

Okay, back to other two idiots. I mean my close friends. Sumit, who loved writing, is a successful Bollywood scriptwriter today. Vatan is a popular cartoonist working with a leading news channel. I am an IAS officer and a writer. We all chased and finally managed to achieve our dreams.

I feel whatever we do, it doesn't matter where and how, we should do it wholeheartedly, with a stress-free mind. Don't let pessimists discourage you.

I'd like to share my favourite poem by **Dushyant Kumar**. This poem has always motivated me. It has always stayed with me during my days of struggle.

'Is nadi ki dhaar se thandi hawa aati to hai,
Naav jarjar hi sahi, lehron se takraati to hai,
Ek chingari kahi se dhoondh laao ae doston
Is diye mein tel se bheegi hui baati to hai.'

(The river sends a cool, gentle breeze,
Though the boat is wrecked,
Yet it faces the challenges of the crashing waves.
We just need a spark, my friend. The lamp still has oil in it.)

SOME SPLENDID SUCCESS STORIES

How my mother made me who I am today

Abhishek Saraf

'Abhishek, why don't you take part in quizzes and competitions? All toppers do. It is a good learning opportunity.'

What could I have told my teachers? That I didn't have the heart to ask my mother to give me some money as entry fee when she was already having difficulty making ends meet? I never spent my pocket money, knowing well that my mother would need it towards the end of the month to somehow keep our heads above water.

This was my childhood. I am Abhishek Saraf. I lost my father to a business feud with his brothers when I was just ten months old. The responsibility of raising me and my then three-year-old elder brother fell on my mother's shoulders. She did not have a job. The struggle of a single Indian mother without any financial security needs no elaboration.

Making it worse was the ongoing litigation with my uncles for our share in the family business. It can be confusing and scary for anyone to navigate judicial proceedings, let alone a woman who cannot read English.

Yet somehow my mother managed to raise me and my brother. Today, my brother is an MBA and works at Google. I'm an IIT Kanpur graduate, ex-Indian Railways Service of Engineers (2013 batch) employee, ex-Indian Revenue

Service (2019 batch) officer and IAS (2020 batch, All India Rank 8 UPSC CSE 2019) officer.

My maternal uncle (Shri Vineet Kumar Jain, IPS) is my rock. He took me to IIT Bombay for counselling after my selection in IIT JEE. My maternal family did more than one can expect. But it was my mother who taught me to stand and walk, to ride a bicycle, who took me to exam centres, from the boards to IIT JEE to ESE 2013 to CSE 2019.

Throughout my childhood people and relatives from my extended family would ask me, 'Son, you don't have a father, how do you feel?' As an adult I realise how painful and insensitive such questions are. Unsurprisingly, their concern never went beyond asking such questions. Truth is, as a child I never had an answer to this question for two reasons. Firstly, I lost my father even before I could learn what having a father was like. For me it was, perhaps, normal. Secondly, my mother did everything within her capacity to ensure that we never felt the absence of our father. It would sound like a movie if I were to list her sacrifices.

As a child, I didn't realise what she went through. But now I see parents struggling to raise their children, impart values to them and make sure they grow up to be responsible adults. I cannot even imagine the fear, anxiety and stress my mother went through. But now as I see how time and circumstances have taken a toll on her, I cannot express in words my gratitude to her for what she did for me.

What she made me is a hardworking, sincere individual who may have an average intelligence quotient but still had the guts to aim for the stars. An individual who could count time and again on his family's unending support in whatever decision he made. Someone who has always been honest with himself and his family regarding whatever path he chose and whatever decision he made. Sincerity, hard work, ambition, family support, perseverance, equanimity, introspection and humility are all that one really needs to achieve whatever success they set out for in life.

Apart from these, I have some traits which my family, especially my mother, nurtured in me. For instance, she always taught me that knowledge never goes to waste. That has made me inquisitive. Inquisitiveness helps me engage sincerely with whatever I study. This enabled me to do well in IIT–JEE and then the Engineering Services exams and Civil Services exam. This, despite my average intellect.

Sometimes people scoff at my average IQ. I can't blame them, as on paper my profile seems stellar. I can speak from my experience of having been in an IIT that apart from the top five hundred rank holders, others are just sincere hardworking students who put in the right effort in the right direction at the right time and were fortunate enough to have all the resources.

Sure, not all of us have all of the above things. But to be fair, only a handful of people have an optimum level of all that is needed—effort, direction, time and resources. Most people have more of one and less of the other. But one can make up for the shortage to some extent. Besides, rather than whining about what life and destiny did not give us, why don't we make the best use of what has been bestowed upon us?

This is what I try to do.

I come from a financially weak background so I borrowed books from seniors in school. And like in many other families, I wore my brother's hand-me-down clothes. I was not sharp, so I worked hard. I never wasted time in superficial relationships, never gossiped and generally tried not to spend time unproductively. When I needed a break from studies, I made sure that my hobbies (like watching documentaries that helped me immensely in my CSE personality test) added to my knowledge and personality.

During my CSE preparation, I didn't score well in the essay paper (105 marks in the first attempt and 79 out of 250 marks in the second). These sub-par scores affected my rank, but patience, perseverance and family's support kept me going. Eventually, all our efforts bore fruit. Even though it's my name in the list, the result belongs to my family, friends, peers and mentors.

Sure, one can argue that luck does play a role. I am not going to deny it. Luck will affect whatever we do. But it is equally true that the harder we work, the luckier we get.

I tell myself regularly where I come from and that a huge responsibility beckons me. What is that? It is the trust of the society and the country. I will discharge my responsibility to the best of my ability, with utmost sincerity. I will seek any and every opportunity to learn and apply what I learn for the benefit of as many as possible. I hope to bring whatever little I can to the society, the nation and the world.

Nishant Jain / 100

Lastly, I would like to say that even though little things cast long shadows at sunset, the sun does rise the next morning and shine for all. As the former president Dr A.P.J. Abdul Kalam said, 'FAIL' means 'First Attempt In Learning', END means 'Effort Never Dies' and NO means 'Next Opportunity'. You can't cross the sea merely by standing and staring at the water. Without your involvement you can't succeed. With your involvement you can't fail.

* * *

The story of a couple who prepared together and achieved success

Aniruddh Kumar

I am from Jahanabad district, Bihar, and I did my schooling at my village. Jahanabad then being a Naxalite zone meant we always lived in the shadow of fear. Fortunately, we had to move to Kanpur because of my father's work. That changed the course of my education. I was a very good student, so expectations from me were high. The pressure of performing well kept me away from sports and extracurricular activities. I still regret that. Extracurricular activities go a long way in personality development.

My goal was simple and straightforward—to complete my engineering and MBA and then work in a multinational company. But an incident changed the direction of my path. Some goons had captured a piece of land my father had bought in Kanpur. It was difficult to fight with them as they were connected to some influential politicians. We contacted the superintendent of police (SP) directly. He listened to us carefully and assured immediate action. True to his words, he initiated action and got my father his land back. It changed my ambition. I started preparing for the Civil Services after completing my engineering.

The beginning was not that bad. I made it past the prelims but didn't go all the way. I turned to the state PCS exams and got selected as Commercial Taxes officer (UPPCS 2012), Assistant Commissioner Commercial Taxes (UPPCS 2013) and DSP (UPPCS 2014). But these were not what I was aiming for.

In 2015 I got married to my old friend Aarti Singh. She was a BDO, but still dreamt of clearing the UPSC. So we decided to merge our dreams. Our strength, courage and desire increased and we adopted a better strategy. Our dedication worked wonderfully and we finally succeeded. Aarti got through the IPS because of AIR 118 and I got AFHQ. I didn't give up and tried again. In 2017 I got AIR 146 and was the topper in Hindi medium.

* * *

An inspiring journey from adversities to opportunities

Ansar Shaikh

I come from a village called Shelgaon in Jalna, Maharashtra. I belong to a lower middle-class family. My father was an auto driver while my mother was a homemaker. Life was not fair to us and we faced many hardships. I was a good student, so, unlike my three siblings, I continued with my studies.

I passed my Class X boards with 76.2 per cent from my village's government school and completed my Class XII boards from Badrinarayan Barwale College, Jalna. By then I had already decided to prepare for the Civil Services. I scored 91.5 per cent in my Class XII boards and went to Pune to pursue graduation in political science from Fergusson College. In the second year of graduation, I started attending coaching classes for UPSC preparation. I completed my graduation in June 2015 with 73 per cent marks. The same year, I appeared for UPSC CSE and I cleared it.

Although I had a habit of working hard, my weak financial background was the biggest hurdle in my journey. There was a time when I did not have money to buy books. Hell, there was a time when I did not have anything to eat the whole day. There was another problem—language. I was preparing in Marathi medium but 60 per cent of my study materials were in English. I had to translate that into Marathi. It was tiring and difficult. But there's always a way. You just have to find it!

I was in Class X when I started dreaming of becoming an IAS officer. Apart from my personal experience, my teacher who had cleared the Maharashtra PSC exam that year was my source of inspiration.

It's true I didn't face any struggle when it comes to cracking the UPSC, but I did face certain adversities. I decided to fight the troubles with a smile, though. I was self-inspired and that's why it was a little easier for me to console myself when I faced problems and bounce back. I believe that the path to success is hidden somewhere in the setbacks. Your failures help you introspect and improve.

I'd like to say that if someone like me, who has faced so many difficulties and deprivations in life, can succeed, anybody can. Nobody has a monopoly on success.

***

When even cerebral palsy cannot deter you from achieving your dreams

Ashish Kumar Verma

Sometimes the past and the future are enclosed in a single moment. For me, it was the moment when doctors told my parents that I had cerebral palsy. They said that I wouldn't be able to walk. Thankfully my IQ wasn't affected.

There was no other option but to accept this harsh truth. Ideally, one should have no qualm accepting the harshest truth. But when the truth collides with regular social norms and standards, struggle is inevitable.

It happened with me. No school in Patna wanted me. Why? Because I was deemed 'abnormal' and hence not elegible to sit with 'normal' kids. But I was determined to fight. It was my deepest wish and my family's greatest support that carved and strengthened the path of my education.

The good thing was that I always topped in my class, whichever school I went to. Also, I loved writing poetry, a passion that is still alive in me. Many of my poems were published in various national and regional magazines. It widened my hope that even I could be useful to society.

The journey of my education was challenging, but the results were great. In the Class XII board (Bihar state board) exams, I secured eighth position in the entire state. I did my graduation and post-graduation from Delhi University in Hindi literature. I ranked third in BA in my university before topping the MA exams. After clearing the NET–JRF exam, I started preparing for the Civil Services. Naturally, it was really difficult to attend coaching classes, so I opted for self-study at home.

My efforts bore fruit in 2011. It was a day of celebration. Various newspapers and news channels were covering the news of my success. I was getting so many congratulatory calls. Among those calls was one from the ministry of social justice and empowerment. They told me that I was the first person in the country who had cracked the UPSC despite cerebral palsy. In 2012, the National Trust, a trust under the auspices of the Ministry of Social Justice and Empowerment, Government of India, honoured me with the **National Award**.

I won't say that my challenges and troubles were over. Because of my physical condition, it was difficult to allot a job to me. Finally, after a year, they allotted me the Indian Defence Accounts Service. Currently I am posted in Patna.

My story is still unfinished; my journey still in progress. When you are different from others, people see you in a different light. We, the society, need to erase this difference. Disability is not a distortion. It's a condition. Everyone has a different physical or mental condition. Then how am I different from everyone else? We, in our own ways, are all complete and incomplete at the same time. I'm wheelchair-bound; you are not. But that doesn't mean I won't have aspirations. I'm sharing one of my poems in translation:

Life is a festival
Let's celebrate it
Every grain of soil is fertile
Try growing a flower

The desire to live
Unweary, intense, resolute, unwavering
Never underestimate
Your resolve

The stars would fall into your hand
Just extend it
Life is a festival
Let's celebrate it.

* * *

How a good command of a language helped me achieve success

Balaji D.K.

You can win over anyone by staying abreast with current affairs. I realised this very early in my life, in fact when I was in Class V. I think I was a wise kid.

One day, angry with me for some reason, my father stopped talking to me. While I sobbed, others watched a quiz programme on TV. However, what made my father happy with me again was that I managed to answer a question on current affairs posed on the programme correctly. He was impressed with my knowledge and hugged me.

This is how my interest in current affairs developed and I realised that I wanted to be an IAS officer.

My teacher, Shri Sachidanand Rao sir, used to say something that motivated me to work towards my dream. He said, 'One should live such a life that people remember you even after death.' This stayed with me. Another teacher, Shri Jagdisharaiya K.S. sir, used to share various success stories of IAS and IPS aspirants with me which strengthened my resolve even more.

Sometimes life also drops hints. When I was waiting for my Class X board results, Shri Jagdish K.J. from my hometown cleared the IAS examination with an all-India 58 rank. I thought I could be the next Jagdish from my town. That is when I formally started to nurture my dreams.

I had scored 100 in mathematics, and got 93.76 per cent overall in my Class X boards. Everybody suggested that I should go for science, but I followed my heart and took up humanities.

I knew that if I had taken up science, it would have offered me various job opportunities in future. I come from a very humble background. My father was from a financially weak family. My grandmother even worked as a labourer. My father did all kinds of odd jobs before he finally joined a Gramin Bank. So it was important for me to find a good job. However, I wanted to follow my dream.

My parents also supported me, though people questioned their decision.

I was in Class XI when I came across a magazine in a bookstore. The cover featured Shri S. Nagarajan (CSE 2005, rank 1). I bought the magazine, but couldn't understand its content as it was in English. I realised I had to improve my command of the language if I wanted to take the IAS exams.

I chalked out a plan. I used to travel 20 kilometres by bus to reach my college. I decided to take buses that played Kannada/Telugu movies. I started translating the movie dialogues. Initially it was difficult, but I kept doing it. I also sought help from my teachers whenever I got stuck. I learnt to think in English. I practised like this for three months. This strategy worked for me.

When I was in Class XII, I started having doubts. What if I couldn't clear the IAS exams? Would I be able to manage my life and career? Should I opt for a professional course? My principal, Shri N.P. Ravindranath ji, came to my rescue. He suggested that I pursue BBA and then MBA. After my MBA, I came to know about a social organisation that offered free boarding, lodging and coaching. However, when I contacted them, they were not so welcoming. But that didn't deter me. Today, I am an IAS officer of Andhra Pradesh cadre. I would suggest all aspiring candidates to not get confused by reading multiple books on one subject. Reading one book twice is any day better than reading two books simultaneously.

* * *

An astonishing journey from a below poverty line (BPL) family to the IAS

Chetan Kumar Meena

On a cold evening of 27 December 2017, I got a call from my baba. He thanked me and said, 'You made me proud, son!'

My selection in the IAS was more important to those who sacrificed a lot to build my future than me. My family was overjoyed at my success.

I was born in a small village called Gajipur in Rajasthan. My parents were farmers and they didn't even know how to use a pen. We were from an economically weak background. But poverty hurts a little less when you live in a joint family. Our family was BPL, so we often got help from the government, which came as a relief.

I did my schooling from a government school in our village. I wanted to study in an IIT, but we couldn't afford the fees. Farming didn't earn us enough. My family had to sell our buffaloes to get some money. I will never forget the day when my mother had to sell her silver ornaments to buy my school uniform. My parents were illiterate, but they always dreamt big for me. They fought life's adversities so that I didn't have to face difficulties.

My dream was to become an IAS officer. To achieve that, I wanted to study in a city like New Delhi, but couldn't afford to spend Rs 10,000 per month. So I decided to stay at home and try to get a job through SSC. My dream came true when I landed a job, as it took care of our financial problem. I was no longer a BPL beneficiary.

I balanced my new job and IAS preparation pretty well. Then, on one fateful day of 2017, my father was diagnosed with final stage lung cancer and we were told that he didn't have much time left. By then, I had cleared the mains and was waiting for an interview call. It was the most stressful phase in my life. It was so difficult for me to continue with my preparation while my father died a little every day.

When I cleared the interview, my father thanked the Almighty and said, 'Son, my dream has come true. I can die in peace now.' He left us after a few days.

I remember another incident following my selection. There was a man in our village who had once insulted and abused me over my caste. However, when I went to touch his feet following my results, he said, 'You made the whole village so proud!'

With my merit I had avenged the old insult.

This reminds me of another incident. As people were celebrating my success and showering me with blessings, I remember embracing an elderly woman from a lower caste who was watching the celebration from a corner. Though some people, especially from a higher caste, gave me a disapproving look, for me it was my first step towards being a responsible IAS officer.

When you are benefitted by government schemes such as MGNREGA, Swachh Bharat, Ujjwala and others, it makes you realise how genuine effort from the government can change your life. As an IAS officer, I will try my best to help needy and poor people through such schemes.

'Jo muskura raha hai, use dard ne paala hoga
Jo chal raha hai, paanv mein uske bhi chhala hoga,
Bina sangharsh ke koi chamak nahin sakta yaaron
Jo jalega, usi diye mein to ujaala hoga.'

(Those who are smiling must have suffered some pain,
Those who are walking must have developed blisters on their soles,
You cannot shine without struggles, my friend
A lamp cannot gleam until it burns.)

* * *

A journey from failure to accomplishment

Gaurav Singh Sogarwal

Village Jagheena, district Bharatpur. I spent all my childhood at a place where farming was the source of living. Even I was involved in farming. When I was a child, my father would tell me success stories of IAS officers, and those fascinating tales instilled the desire in me to become one. To be able to serve the people and the nation kind of became a mission for me.

My father was a teacher and my mother a homemaker. It's true that I grew up in a rural environment, but education was never ignored in our family. My elder sister did her post-graduation in Zoology. My younger brother completed his MBA and is now working in a multinational company in Bangalore. But my father always wanted me to become an IAS officer. I lost him before I could fulfil his dream, though. His loss made me even more determined. I had to do this for my father.

I did my engineering from Pune and accepted a job just to overcome financial constraints. I worked there for three years before arriving in Delhi in 2013.

Balancing studies and family responsibilities was not easy. I found myself inclined towards spirituality. It gave me solace. The Bhagavad Gita and my connection with ISKCON acted as guiding forces.

On my first attempt, I missed my chance in the prelims by just one mark. I missed another chance, the next time in the mains, just because of that one mark. But I trusted my determination and spirituality. Meanwhile, I got selected as an assistant commandant in the BSF, so finances were not a problem.

For my third attempt, I focused primarily on my writing skills. I made a study plan where newspapers played a very significant role. It helped me improve my general knowledge. So, naturally, I scored better in general studies. I also worked on essay-writing. Finally I succeeded and got through to the Uttar Pradesh cadre.

It is good to tighten your grip over current affairs. Spirituality and reading biographies of great people can be helpful for your personality development. Try to follow the famous doctorine of nishkama karma from the Gita. It helped me at every step of my life.

***

A farmer's daughter to an IPS officer

Ilma Afroz

I am from Moradabad, a place famous for brass handicrafts.

My father was a farmer. Our school session used to begin in April. After selling wheat at the government rate, papa would rush to town to buy books and stationary for me. I didn't know the full form of MSP, i.e., Minimum Support Price, but I always got my books. I always tagged along whenever my father went to the collectorate or the SDM office for work.

Everything was going well till I lost my father when I was just fourteen. Maa brought us up single-handedly. People often told her, 'Don't over-pamper your daughter. Don't give her so much freedom. She's going to get married eventually.' But she never gave in to the pressure.

My mother always taught me to fight back, no matter how difficult the situation was. She taught me to work hard, move ahead with confidence, but stay grounded. She used to tell me, 'Trouble is inevitable. Try to be like Arjun (in the Mahabharata) and stay focused.'

Once I went to the collectorate for some scholarship-related work. The orderly, in his white uniform, standing outside the office, stopped me and asked me to come again with a guardian. I ignored him and went inside. The district magistrate smiled, signed my form and said, 'Ilma, you should join the Civil Services.'

My educational journey is pretty long. I did my graduation in philosophy from Delhi's St Stephen's College. Those were the three best years of my life. I participated in the philosophy committee meetings, wrote papers and learnt the theories of *anekantavada* and *syadvada*. During my university days, I learnt about karmayoga in Indian philosophy.

I did my post-graduation from Oxford University. Studying at Oxford made me understand different perspectives of people who came from all over the world. I learnt to get inspired by new, diverse thoughts. Then I got the opportunity to work in New York City.

Amidst the glamour of New York, I missed my family. My mother was alone. She needed me. Why did I study so much? Why did I get higher education? To be part of another country's growth? Eventually, I decided to come back to my motherland.

Encouraged by my brother, I took the Civil Services exam. I secured the rank of 217 and got into the IPS (Himachal Pradesh cadre).

I would advise you to keep your preparation simple. It's good to stay updated about current affairs. Going to the library is a very good habit. Be selective when choosing books to read. Many aspirants create a tall pile of books while preparing. It's not a good idea.

One more thing. When I was at St Stephen's, I had read '*Satyamev Jayate Nanritam*' (Truth alone triumphs, not falsehood) written in bold in the college auditorium. It always guides me.

***

An inspiring journey from the hills

Kanchan Kandpal

Words often fail to express emotions. I experienced that on 31 May 2017, when, on a pleasant evening in Nainital, I saw my name in a PDF file of the UPSC final results. The designation of an IAS officer was a dream, and life had bestowed this upon me.

There was a decent educational environment in my house, so I always scored the highest in my exams. I passed the Class XII boards with flying colours and pursued BTech from Pant Nagar University. After completing my BTech in 2015, I had a job through campus placement but all I was thinking was how I could make my life relevant. The relevance of our lives depends on our contribution to our society and nation. Right, then, the Civil Services it had to be. In the quest for good books and guidance, I reached Delhi.

Every aspirant has some kind of fear. Mine was preparing with Hindi as my medium. Everybody said that it would be difficult to crack UPSC in Hindi. But I decided to fight my fears. After all, some fighters have achieved this target—Mr Nishant Jain, Mr Prem Sukh Delu and Ms Ira Singhal were inspirations to me.

'De di chunauti Sindhu ko
Tab dhaar kya, majhdhaar kya?'

(If you have challenged the vast river and set your boat to sail and steer into it, don't worry about the angry waves or the lurching boat.)

I followed these inspiring lines by Harivansh Rai Bachchan and decided to fight it out. To be very frank, preparing in Hindi turned out to be a strong point for me. In 2016, I cracked the UPPCS prelims in March, the UPSC prelims in August and the Rajasthan Civil Services in September. In January 2017, I passed Uttarakhand's PSC (UKPSC) preliminary examination. In May 2017, I got through IPS with a rank of 263. I had finally managed to defeat fear that prevents many small-town youth to dream big.

It has been proven by many that if we make a good study plan and keep trying with determination, we can achieve success. I'd like to say:

Uchaayiaan agar buland ho
To maujood hain raaste
Hamein to nikalna hai bas
Tarakki ke vaaste.

(If your spirit is high
You'll find a way
We just have to set off
To achieve success.)

***

A government school student who became an IPS officer

Md Mustaque

'People with passion can change the world.'

When I was a kid, I read these words of Steve Jobs somewhere. At that time, these were mere words to me. But now when I think about it, I realise they mean much more. They have the power to change your life. My success revolves around this stubbornness.

I come from a very simple, rural family in a Bihar village where there was no electricity. I did my schooling from a government school and graduated from Patna University in 2008 through correspondence. I wanted to become an IAS officer since Class XII. But there was no one who could guide me, who could tell me about the preparation. Even my family was not so confident about my aspirations.

My journey started with failure. Many of my friends had joined the army just after Class X. So I, too, decided to appear for the NDA but failed in that exam. English was my weak point.

But this failure made me more determined, almost stubborn. I decided to appear for the Civil Services exam. When I was just twenty-one, I appeared for the prelims without preparing for the mains. I cleared the prelims on the first attempt. This made me feel like I had already become an IAS officer. That overconfidence was my biggest mistake. I failed to clear the mains, which was inevitable.

I was very disheartened when I failed the 2011 CSAT prelims. The future seemed bleak. Everything was so stressful and my confidence was sinking like a wrecked ship. I would just sit alone in a park or talk to myself. Family pressure was not helping either. They were expecting me to pick up some job. Thankfully, they didn't discourage me completely. My teachers, friends and family helped me come out of this gloomy pessimism. I appeared for the CPF in 2011 and got selected in the first attempt. This success perked up my confidence and helped me bounce back. The next year, I tried for the UPSC again. This time my preparation was better and eventually I got allotted to the Indian Revenue Service (IRS). It was a pleasant surprise because I wasn't expecting it.

But, thanks to my stubbornness, I refused to give up. I tried again, and in 2015 I got selected for the IPS.

* * *

IAS officer at twenty-three, that too without any coaching

Pooja Parth

I grew up with five siblings. My father is a librarian at a medical college, so we were surrounded by books.

I studied at a local school till Class X. After that, my father got me enrolled at the Government Polytechnic College, Kota, in electronics and communications.

After that, in 2011, I decided to pursue graduation from Janki Devi Bajaj Girls' College. I appeared in the patwari examination but couldn't secure a place. I did my graduation in history with sociology and philosophy as pass subjects. When I was in my third year, I again wrote the patwari exam and succeeded. But I decided not to join.

I wanted to be a civil servant. My father was a guiding force, encouraging me to read well. He always taught me about the importance of being independent.

I pursued master's in sociology. At the same time, I started preparing for general studies and mathematics short tricks. To increase my knowledge of current affairs, I used to read newspapers and competitive magazines. In 2013, I appeared for the Rajasthan State Services (pre) exams. In 2014, I was preparing for the final exam of my post-graduation when I appeared for the IAS (pre). I did not waste time, got back to academics and focused on my MA, just in case I didn't clear the prelims. It's important to be prepared, you know. And time—that's one thing you shouldn't waste.

After clearing the prelims I started reading editorials to polish my opinionated mind.

For essay writing, I didn't prepare any particular topic. But there has to be a chronological order while writing an essay so that it is relevant and crisp. A popular magazine called *Pratiyogita Darpan* taught me to write good, effective essays. I learnt that a good essay should have an intriguing start, a body that covers different aspects of that topic and a striking end.

For the interview, I focused on current affairs and practised how to express my opinion coherently and effectively. Since I had never appeared in any interview before, I set up mock interview sessions with my father.

My interview was with Hemchand Gupta sir's board. They asked various diverse questions about my DAF (Detailed Application Form) form, the Gurjar agitation, the National Judicial Commission, on lowering the age of juvenile criminals, the effect of television serials on society, the Kashmir issue, the role of the media during the 26/11 terrorist attacks, etc. This is how I completed my whole preparation and achieved success without any professional coaching.

I got the rank of 163 in the 2014 Civil Services exam. I got selected for the IAS, Rajasthan cadre.

* * *

Cracked UPSC during pregnancy

Dr Pragya Jain

Everyone has a unique temperament and personality. Everyone has some good qualities and faults. This is what determines their identity.

According to Robert S. Woodworth, an American psychologist who developed the world's first personality test, 'Personality is the mirror of human behaviour, which can be exhibited through one's style of expressing views, style of working, interests and philosophical views about life.'

But our personality cannot develop overnight. It's a continuous process. Our family, society, education, experiences and opinion play a significant role in personality building. My personality is also the result of the exciting and challenging journey of my life.

I completed my primary education in a small town called Baraut. It's a municipal board in Bagpat district, Uttar Pradesh. My father is an Ayurvedic doctor and my mother a graduate from Delhi University. They were very serious about our education from the very beginning. I got state level ranks in Class X and XII boards.

People's pain and helplessness make me restless and that is why I decided to be a doctor. I started practising in Baraut and then opened a clinic in Delhi after I got married. I worked with dedication and tried my level best to help the poor and needy. But after some years, I felt that this platform was small, the resources were limited. This is how my fascination for UPSC grew.

I cleared the prelims and mains on my first attempt but I lost my chance in the interview by just a few marks. The second time, I couldn't even clear the prelims because of bad health and a stressed mind. Despite being on bed rest during my pregnancy, I didn't give up and prepared for my third attempt. This time, I went all the way and got selected for the IPS.

My uniform has given me a golden opportunity to create social awareness and express my patriotism. But the challenge was not over. Not yet. It was hard to keep my six-month-old daughter away from me during my training. Moreover, after pregnancy, our body takes time to get back to normal. So, naturally, it was difficult to match the level of exercise. I fractured both my hands while cycling but my optimism and courage were intact. They helped me face the challenges fearlessly and find the right direction.

Everyone is special in their own way. Everyone has their own qualities. Your path and direction depend on your perspective and state of mind.

* * *

A student who became an assistant professor at twenty-three!

Prashant Raman Ravi

I was born in a small village called Patilaar in Pashchim Champaran, Bihar. Yes, the same Pashchim Champaran where Mahatma Gandhi had started his Satyagraha movement.

My childhood was happy and carefree. I studied in a government school where we used to sit on jute sacks.

My father was a farmer, an educated one too. Life was going great till a fateful day when I came to know that my mother had urinary tract cancer. I was too young to understand what that was but I knew it was a dangerous disease and treatment was very expensive. I had known that there was some problem with my mother's health as papa would take her for treatment regularly. But I didn't know it was so serious until then.

But it seemed like it would be better soon. Maa always said she was okay. 'Nothing will happen to me. I have small kids to look after. I have to live for them.'

I had always believed my mother's words. So I believed her then too.

I had always wondered about my father's work. How could a first-class postgraduate like him not get a decent job? I asked him once. He smiled. 'I did get a job. But then there was a 100 per cent chance to get a government teacher's job, so I left it. Unfortunately, there was some problem and I didn't get the teacher's job,' he said.

The case was pending at the Supreme Court. Two good things happened in 2012. After a long legal struggle, my father finally got his job. And, to our immense relief, my mother defeated cancer. It was a victory of her faith.

I was a BA final year student then. The last few years were so difficult that sometimes I thought I wouldn't be able to complete my education. But my mother's faith in me was so strong that I kept going.

Amidst all the struggles, I passed my Class X boards in 2008 with flying colours. I was quite an active student in school. Be it sports, cultural programmes, singing or poetry recitation, I never missed a chance to participate.

In college, I wanted to study humanities but couldn't go ahead with it. It was a general perception that humanities was for weak students and those who were intelligent always chose science. I chose science. There was no pressure from my family. It was purely my decision, of course, triggered by my own fears and prejudice.

Soon I realised that it was a mistake, as I didn't enjoy studying science. Still I worked hard and managed 60 per cent marks. It was such a great relief. In 2010, I appeared for the BHU entrance test and got selected. I chose my favourite subject—Hindi literature. When you choose subjects that interest you, studying becomes an enjoyable journey.

The body language of my professors and the way they used to connect with the youth quite fascinated me, but the appeal of IAS was something else. I was in a state of confusion and then one of my professors from Patna Universiy, Matuknath Chaudhary, came to my rescue and cleared my confusion. 'Both these professions are prestigious. They are both respectable and significant mediums to serve your society. Just make sure whatever you choose to do, it should make you happy and fulfilled. Something that interests you and makes your life beautiful,' he said.

His words touched my heart and I realised that according to my nature and interest, becoming a professor would be more suitable and fulfilling. When I asked maa, she said, 'Do whatever you want to do. I'm with you, always.' Her words wiped off the remaining mist of confusion. I recharged myself with new determination and energy and slowly got very passionate about my career as a professor. Consequently, my passion fetched me a gold medal and I got selected for UGC NET in 2015 while doing my master's.

I got selected for MPhil at Delhi University. I cannot forget to mention my elder brother Mr Hemant Raman Ravi who constantly inspired and guided me. While I was doing my MPhil, I came to know about the vacancy of an assistant professor's post in Himachal Pradesh University. I filled up the form and started preparing. I performed extremely well in the written test and got the interview call.

'You're too young for this post. You don't look like a professor,' one of the board members said in the interview room. I didn't know how to react, so I just said thank you. The interview was going well.

'You're from Bihar, so why did you choose Himachal Pradesh University? It's quite far from your place,' said another board member.

'Sir, teaching is not just a job for me. It's my passion. For me, it's the best form of expressing myself. So, distance doesn't matter at all,' I answered, and they looked satisfied. I secured a place in the final list.

I got the appointment letter. It was a result of my hard work, dedication and my mother's faith. The day I joined the Himachal Pradesh University as assistant professor, I was just twenty-three years and two months old. I have learnt the art of finding joy even in my struggles from my mother. I have inherited her rock solid faith. She taught me to stay positive in adverse situations.

* * *

Smart study will help you achieve success

Rajat Saklecha

If you have watched the movie *Jab We Met*, you would be familiar with a place called Ratlam. Ratlam is quite popular for good quality salted snacks and designer gold ornaments. This is where I completed my schooling.

My father works with the SBI. There are five more members in my family—a younger brother, my parents and grandparents. Small-town boys are also like 'paraya dhan' (wealth that belongs to someone else). One day they leave home in the quest for better opportunities and a better future. I did my engineering from Indore and then left for Delhi to fulfil my dream of becoming an IAS officer. I started in 2012, and I achieved one level at a time—the prelims on my second attempt, mains the next time and then the interview the following year.

I was very fond of reading newspapers. It helped me improve my general knowledge at an early age. I felt I needed to do something for society, hence opted for the Civil Services. Plus, it was the best way to make my family happy and proud.

Hard work is crucial, of course, but success is not just about hard work. There are several other factors. Moral support of family and friends, your ability to beat disappointments and accept rejections and attitude to move ahead with optimism, all of these work wonders. Just a few steps more, I used to think, and this thought led me to success.

If you are preparing for the Civil Services, it's important to understand the things around you with an analytical approach. To achieve this, reading newspapers, magazines, websites like Quora and Wikipedia and relevant information on Google is extremely helpful. To express your knowledge on a certain platform is a good idea and for that, websites like Insightsonindia and IASbaba are useful. Writing questions and answering queries on these websites is an interesting exercise. I had mostly studied online, as coaching notes seemed tiring to me. However, if you read the notes carefully and smartly, it saves your time. So, what I mean to say is that don't look for multiple sources for a single thing. Keep revising what you have learnt. I believe that even seven-eight hours of dedicated study per day is enough. Try to be consistent. Do not break the routine you have developed.

Achieving success in the Civil Services brings immense respect, so much that I cannot explain in words. In fact, it creates a path for you if you want to achieve something significant, find meaning in your life or want to contribute to the society and the nation.

If you are true to yourself, if your efforts are genuine and if you're walking on the right path, 'Nothing can stop you but yourself' (Liam Lini song).

* * *

The story of a technocrat-turned-bureaucrat

Rahul Gupta

I was born and raised in Shivpuri, Madhya Pradesh. My father is a sub-engineer in Sarva Shiksha Abhiyan in Rajgarh (MP).

I cracked the JEE from Kota after dropping a year post Class XII. I have done BTech and MTech from IIT Delhi in electrical engineering. I started studying for UPSC CSE in 2013. Initially, it was difficult to manage because I was preparing with English as my medium in spite of my Hindi medium background. When I picked up NCERT (English medium) books for the first time, I found it a little difficult to comprehend the language. Moreover, managing the UPSC preparation and my college projects simultaneously was quite hectic. Also, the syllabus of engineering and UPSC are very varied, and coming from an engineering background, it was difficult to develop a genuine interest in the UPSC syllabus and study in-depth.

During my final year, my mind was in a state of imbroglio. I realised that I would be happy in life if I saw any tangible impact of my work. Additionally, I wanted a job where common sense, rather than theoretical knowledge, was applied. Civil services seemed the best option at that time.

I couldn't clear the mains on my first attempt. I was disappointed and disheartened. But after an honest introspection, I found that there were some areas where my preparation needed more focus and attention. My second attempt certainly required a greater effort. I have appeared for the CSE thrice. The second time, I got the rank of 306. I was not satisfied, so I tried again. Next time, I got the rank of 182 and cracked the IPS.

The list of books is common for almost 90 per cent of candidates who have cleared this exam. Anyone can find recommendations on the blogs of selected candidates. But just picking several books is not enough. Understanding the syllabus and the content is more important. The questions are very dynamic and based on current affairs, so a thorough knowledge and understanding of the topics is going to be very useful. Overall, you have to be hardworking and consistent. Choose your optional subject wisely, as it's crucial to be an expert in your own subject.

Do what makes you happy because only then can you attain excellence and live a happy life. Be the master of your own destiny; carve out your own path. Failures are part of life. Accept them gracefully and learn from them.

* * *

Conquering troubles and overcoming scarcities

Ratan Deep Gupta

There's a small town called Nawabganj in Gonda district, Uttar Pradesh. That's my hometown where I grew up with two siblings. I am the eldest. My father had a small shop in the town.

As I grew up, my grades and our financial condition started declining. I got 66 per cent in the Class X boards. In the Class XII boards, I got 51 per cent.

Income was negligible after we had to close the shop for unavoidable reasons. I couldn't pay my fees. Our electricity was disconnected. Even managing proper meals was getting tougher day by day. I didn't know what to do. I got the job of a tutor. It paid me only Rs 100 but it was the turning point of my life because I used that money to buy a magazine called *Pratiyogita Darpan*. I read some success stories in that magazine and they got me thinking. If others could succeed, why couldn't I? I felt that I could certainly change my life if I worked really hard.

Thus started my UPSC journey. My friends were kind enough to pay my fees and I took up a teaching job at a local school, for which I got Rs 600 per month. To support my family, I sold candles and flags at the roadside. I got some time at night that I dedicated to studies.

I got the job of an accountant at the SBI through SSC. I thought this success was going to make my journey easy, but I was wrong. I couldn't clear the mains on my first attempt. The second time, I couldn't even pass the prelims because of a very serious ailment. Because of my sickness, working and studying together was getting really difficult. When I was terribly disappointed by my recurring failures, it was my family and friends who helped me improve my confidence. That's why family and friends are special. But I got rejected in the interview in my fourth and fifth attempts. Disappointment was gripping me. But my sister still had faith in my talent and capacity for hard work. She used to encourage me with a beautiful quote:

'Koshish kar hal niklega
Aaj nahin to kal niklega
Arjun ke teer sa sadh
Maruthal se bhi jal niklega.'

(Try,
You will find a way
Tomorrow, if not today.
Stay focused
like Arjun's dart,
The water will spurt out of the desert.)

And her inspiring words worked for me. Finally I cracked the Civil Services exam. Currently, I am an officer of the Indian Railway Traffic Service (IRTS).

I'd like to conclude my story with a thought—any competition is not just the test of your knowledge. It is also a test of your perseverance, patience and endurance. Sometimes it is important to burn in the fire of struggle so you can emerge shining like gold.

Your circumstances can be unfavourable. That's life, but don't let the shadow of despair overpower you. Whenever you feel gloomy, remind yourself of these lines:

'What's so special about that path;
Why should one admire
the ability of the wayfarer
if there's no hurdle on his way?
A sailor's patience is tested
If reverse waves don't leave him in dismay.'

* * *

Hard work never goes in vain

Sachin Jain

I am from Baraut, a small town in Bagpat district, Uttar Pradesh. My father is an accountant and mother a homemaker. I completed my studies at a Hindi medium school. I was very good at mathematics, so I tried for engineering and got admission in IET, Lucknow. Selection was easy but learning English and computers was a challenge. I got a job in Wipro, Hyderabad through campus selection. So I was kind of settled, but there was tremendous work pressure. It was tiring but that pressure made me realise something: If I could work so hard then why couldn't I try for the best job of India?

This thought gradually turned into a burning desire and I left the job. I came to Delhi and started preparing for the UPSC exams. I cleared the prelims on my very first attempt but then I failed four consecutive exams. Fortunately, I got a job in United India Insurance Company, Indore.

Financially, I was stable. Plus, in this job, I got plenty of time, so I started teaching students preparing for the Civil Services. During this period I made many notes from various kinds of books. Then one day, something totally unexpected happened. The government extended two attempts in the Civil Services exam. I took leave and came to Delhi again.

My hard work paid off. In 2014 I got the all-India rank of 714. I didn't lose hope and tried again. That was my last chance and I aced it with the rank of 286, and got the IRS. It was a tough journey, full of disappointments and surprises, but most importantly, it was a learning experience.

I'd like to say something to all aspiring candidates. Read the standard books at least thrice. Make a habit of writing daily. Don't waste your time in thinking about best coaching centres or best books/websites or the best strategy for preparation. Research well and start preparing. Make notes before going to bed. It gives you something to look forward to for the next day. Stop overthinking. If you are honest and hardworking, believe me, success cannot stay away from you.

* * *

He didn't stop even after losing his eyesight in childhood

Satender Singh

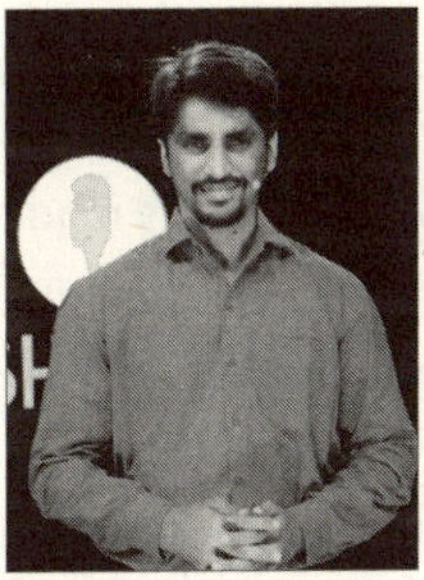

I was born in Amroha district in Uttar Pradesh. When I was just eighteen months old, I got pneumonia and because of a wrong injection, I lost my sight forever. When I grew up, I became conscious of my weakness. I desperately wanted to defeat my friends in sports. Maybe this was my way to beat my weakness and to dissipate the effects of blindness.

I wanted to study just like my friends. I used to listen to them, learning the alphabet and tables, and memorised them before my friends.

My friends always helped me at the playground. Sometimes they used a ball that made sound so that I could play and sometimes they would declare me the referee so that I could handle the arguments. I realised one thing—children are more supportive than grown-ups.

My parents didn't get a chance to study when they were young. My mother couldn't read or write and my father managed to study till Class V. They were terribly worried about my education but didn't know how to teach a visually impaired child. One of my uncles lived and worked in Delhi. One day, he was travelling in a DTC bus when he witnessed something astonishing. There was a blind boy in the bus and he was able to tell time by touching his watch. My uncle hesitated a little but ultimately asked the boy how he did it. He found he studied at a school for blind children. That was the turning point of my life. That school changed my life.

Blind schools use certain techniques to teach. I learnt Braille and then I learnt to work on the computer. I used to read, or rather, listen to recorded audio books. This school gave me a new life. It taught me to be independent. It made me realise that nothing is impossible.

One thing strikes me whenever I think about my life is that even a small incident can bring a big change. If my uncle hadn't seen that boy on the bus I wouldn't have found my school. Maybe I would have been a blind farmer, desperately trying be smart in front of his friends.

When I was in Class XII, I heard a lot about Delhi University's St Stephen's College. I really wanted to study there. I was fortunate enough to get admission there. Mine had been a vernacular language medium school while the college was completely English medium. I was not very good at English. By the time I could understand one sentence, our teachers would move to the fifth or sixth sentence. I tried to speak in English but many of my classmates mocked me. Some of my friends tried to be sympathetic and suggested I should quit college and complete my education in a Hindi medium college. But my dream was to study at St Stephen's.

I found a way to deal with my language problem. I downloaded NCERT books in English that I had read in Hindi. I slowly started to understand the lectures. Some teachers even praised me.

I did my masters from JNU in political science and international relations. I had always wanted to be a professor and I got the opportunity in 2015 when I got selected as an ad hoc assistant professor at Shri Aurobindo College. I'm still teaching. I enjoy it immensely. But sometimes I felt a sense of emptiness, like something was missing. I felt that I needed a more diverse identity so that I could bring positive changes in society. I had seen so many stereotypes, prejudices and biases about blindness since my childhood. I wanted to break those shackles. So I appeared for the Civil Services.

I didn't succeed the first time. I blame my carelessness. The second time, I managed to clear the prelims but missed the interview by nine marks. It was the fault of my ailment. I cracked it on my third attempt with the rank of 714. Now

I feel that I could have secured a better rank, so I'm going to try again with all my mind.

I would like to say that we all have certain flaws and limitations. Make sure that they don't act as hurdles in your path.

* * *

A journey of success through passion and vivacity

Sukirti Madhav

Watching cattle grazing while dusting off my shorts and shabby shirt; playing with my friends the whole day; picking a story book from a dusty pile and reading it in a single sitting; running after a flying kite or chasing sparrows; fishing and picking berries; carrying the food for my father to the farm and then taking a bath at the tube well. This is how I spent my childhood.

Then I grew up and completed my graduation and MBA. In 2010, I got a job at Coal India right after finishing my MBA. 2010 was memorable for one more reason. My father's job was reinstated after a twenty-two-year-long legal battle. However, these twenty-two years had taught us a lot of things. My parents became farmers, suffered scarcity and faced troubles but they always motivated me to dream big.

I belong to a small village called Malaypur in Jamui district, Bihar. Civil services is quite popular among Biharis. So naturally, I had heard a lot about it. My father always wanted me to prepare for the Civil Services seriously so that I would get through, but I considered myself an average student, so I decided to stay away.

I was happy. Months rolled on, but somewhere something was pricking. So many questions were churning in my mind—Do I belong somewhere else? Do I deserve better? Can I live a more meaningful life? Should I dream big and chase that dream—the dream that my father dreamt for me? A strange kind of restlessness gripped me.

I couldn't afford to leave my job, and preparing for the UPSC exam (without coaching) was very difficult. I was so unsure. Should I leave everything and go for it? At least once? Years later, would I regret not giving it a shot? I emerged from this dilemma with a concrete decision, and that's how my UPSC journey began—with all my strength, energy and enthusiasm. My determination strengthened day by day. It was not a smooth journey but my troubles actually inspired me. I got IRS on my first attempt and IPS the next time. I dreamt big. I trusted my ability, worked hard and started a journey in which my family's support never left me. This journey found its destination at a very beautiful, satisfying place.

Friends, dare to dream and aim big. Trust your abilities and be confident. Work hard. This is what you need to succeed.

'Dekhe jo sapne peechha kar,
Hadon ko apne kheencha kar
Beeti taahi bisaar ke
Naye sapnon ki baat to kar
Manzil to mil hi jaayegi
Ek kadam badha, shuruaat to kar.'

(Dare to dream and chase it
Widen your horizon
Forget your past
And talk about new dreams
Your destination will embrace you
Take a step, and start.)

***

An IAS officer from a tribal belt

Suresh Kumar Jagat

I am from a village called Parsada in Korba district, Chhattisgarh. It's a tribal village situated at Maikal Hills. I have always been a brilliant student and maybe that's the reason I could go out of my village with dreams in my eyes. My education was really difficult till high school. Certain classes in our school had no teachers. I studied in a janbhagidaari school. As is obvious from the name, these schools are run with the support of people. I completed my high school somehow and passed with 90 per cent marks.

What about further studies? It was a big question. My brothers helped me get admission to Bilaspur's Bharat Maata School. Studying was not easy but I passed my Class XII boards with flying colours, ranking fifth in the state. What's the main problem of students who study in village schools? What's the reason of their low confidence? English and maths. That's why I focused on these two subjects. I cleared AIEEE and got admission to NIT Raipur. I passed my mechanical engineering degree with 81 per cent marks.

I am a farmer's son, so financial security was my primary concern. I secured a place in ONGC through campus selection and got through GATE to join NTPC. I was not ready for the Civil Services exam, so I worked for three years. After that I gathered courage to sit for the exams. I passed the Indian Engineering Services and joined the Central Water Commission in Bhubaneshwar. My dream to go to Delhi for UPSC preparations still remained unfulfilled.

I tried it twice while working. I took the exam in Hindi. Then I decided to try in English. Since I wasn't staying in Delhi, the internet was my saviour. I started preparing in English, with geography as my special subject. I tasted success in 2016, getting IRTS. But I didn't give up, as I thought I could do better and tried again. I got IAS on my fourth attempt. I achieved it with a full-time job and without any coaching.

I wondered why I failed initially, and I realised that my overconfidence was a problem. Also, I didn't practise essays and the ethics paper. I didn't write my answers while preparing. Anyway, we learn from our mistakes.

Success tastes sweeter when you achieve it fighting adversities. It has a certain charm.

* * *

Struggle makes you stronger

Ummul Kher

I was born in a village called Sojat in Pali district, Rajasthan. I lived with my mother, elder sister and elder brother. My mother belonged to an educated, Kashmiri family. My father left us for Delhi when I was just ten months old. My mother started teaching at a local school. In a patriarchal society, a single mother has to struggle every day. My mother couldn't take it. She eventually lost her job. I was sent to my father and new mother when I was just five.

Even my father's financial condition was not very sound. He couldn't even buy me pens and notebooks. So, when I was in Class VII, I started taking tuitions. My stepmother didn't want me to study. She believed that it was better to learn sewing and stitching after Class V so that I could do something 'useful' at home. Every year I'd tell her, 'Just this year. Next year, I'll leave school.'

I completed Class VIII somehow. They didn't allow me to continue studies and decided to send me back to Rajasthan. I took a tough decision to leave them and stay at a rented house with the money earned through tuitions. It was a very tough decision at that age, but I couldn't imagine my life without proper education.

I was too busy struggling to think about the Civil Services. My main focus was on completing my education so that I could get a decent job. I got involved in social service, fought for the rights of blind people and got several opportunities to travel the world to lead this movement. I completed my master's from JNU and then qualified for NET–JRF. By now, my financial condition was much better, so I decided to try for UPSC, and fortunately, I cracked it on my very first attempt.

I never faced any difficulty during my preparation, except time management. I knew that I wouldn't be able to appear for the Civil Services again and again. So I became too self-disciplined, almost a recluse. Later, I realised it was a mistake because I didn't get any feedback and lost the chance to rectify my mistakes. I would suggest you to make some time for yourself. Don't be too hard on yourself. It can make you restless. Do spend some time in activities you enjoy. Exercise or take a walk. Always remember, if you make a strategy that involves self-discipline, hard work and wisdom, your success is guaranteed.

I cracked the UPSC in 2017 and am currently working as an IRS officer.

* * *

A journey from a constable to a police officer

Vijay Singh Gurjar

I come from a village called Devipura, Jhunjhnu in Rajasthan. My father is a farmer and my mother a homemaker. I have four siblings. I studied in a local government school and was an average student. After Class X, my father got me enrolled in a Sanskrit school because he believed that it would be easier to get a job as a Sanskrit teacher.

After my graduation, I started preparing for jobs but couldn't land any. In 2009, there were vacancies for constables in the Delhi Police. One of my friends was already a policeman and he suggested to me to come to Delhi and take coaching for the exam. I got selected.

Like a regular middle class boy, I also aspired to crack the IAS or the IPS. After a few days, I got selected for the post of sub-inspector. This success boosted my confidence and I decided to start preparations for the Civil Services.

I appeared for the SSC graduate level exam. After my training, I was posted at Sangam Vihar Police Station, Delhi, for a year. We had to work fifteen to sixteen hours a day. It was difficult to devote time for my studies. I received my SSC result after around ten months. I was posted to the

Central Excise Custom and Service Tax department, Kerala. I resigned from the Delhi Police and joined my job in Kerala. Here I managed some time for my studies. Preparing alone was a bit discouraging, though.

I re-appeared for SSC and this time I got the post of Income Tax Inspector because of my better rank. I joined in February 2014. Now that I was again in Delhi, I enrolled myself in a coaching class but didn't like their methods. So I decided to study on my own. I tried thrice but couldn't even clear the prelims. Meanwhile, my family was putting pressure on me to get married because I was already engaged since 2012. So I got married in 2015. My wife was very supportive. She and one of my friends always encouraged and motivated me. They helped me work on my weaknesses. I got an interview call in 2016 but I again failed to crack the Civil Services.

I was so disheartened and agitated that I thought of selling my books. Just when I was losing all hope, my wife, Sunita, told me to try one last time. 'Just four months,' she said. 'You have worked so hard. Just try one more time.'

I worked on my flaws and this time I got selected with a rank of 574. I was the first person to crack the Civil Services in my village and all the fifteen adjacent villages combined.

I got an opportunity to work for people in need. I have seen their troubles.

I would like to end my story with these words:

'Zindagi ki asli udaan abhi baaki hai
Iradon ke imtehaan abhi baaki hai
Abhi to naapi hai mutthi bhar zameen,
Abhi to saara aasmaan baaki hai.'

(I have yet to take the real flight of life
I have yet to take real test of life
I have just measured a fistful of land
I have yet to travel the sky so grand.)